The
Performing Arts
in a New Era

Kevin F. McCarthy | Arthur Brooks | Julia Lowell | Laura Zakaras

RAND

Supported by The Pew Charitable Trusts

The research in this report was supported by the The Pew Charitable Trusts.

Library of Congress Cataloging-in-Publication Data

The performing arts in a new era / Kevin McCarthy ... [et al.].
    p. cm.
    "MR-1367."
    Includes bibliographical references.
    ISBN 0-8330-3041-8
    1. Performing arts—United States. I. McCarthy, Kevin, 1945–

PN2266.5 .P475 2001
791'.0973'09051—dc21

                                                    2001048134

RAND is a nonprofit institution that helps improve policy and decisionmaking through research and analysis. RAND® is a registered trademark. RAND's publications do not necessarily reflect the opinions or policies of its research sponsors.

Cover design by Eileen Delson La Russo

Published 2001 by RAND
1700 Main Street, P.O. Box 2138, Santa Monica, CA 90407-2138
1200 South Hayes Street, Arlington, VA 22202-5050
201 North Craig Street, Suite 102, Pittsburgh, PA 15213
RAND URL: http://www.rand.org/
To order RAND documents or to obtain additional information, contact
Distribution Services: Telephone: (310) 451-7002; Fax: (310) 451-6915;
Email: order@rand.org

The Pew Charitable Trusts commissioned *The Performing Arts in a New Era* from RAND in 1999 as part of a broad initiative aimed at increasing policy and financial support for nonprofit culture in the United States. The goal of this study was to assist us in bringing new and useful information to the policy debate about the contributions and needs of the cultural sector at the national, state, and local levels.

The study was inspired in part by a pair of landmark reports on the performing arts published during the mid-1960s: *The Performing Arts: Problems and Prospects, the Rockefeller Panel Report on the Future of Theatre, Dance, Music in America* (1965); and the Twentieth Century Fund's report, *Performing Arts—The Economic Dilemma,* by William J. Baumol and William G. Bowen (1966). These reports described the burgeoning landscape of the nonprofit professional performing arts in the United States, articulating their benefits to American society and calling for a level of governmental and philanthropic support sufficient to their needs. Both reports noted that it was appropriate, at a time when the industrial economy of the United States had grown and prospered and the material needs of its citizens were by and large being met, for the nation to turn its attention to nonmaterial values—what would now be characterized as quality-of-life concerns—including the emotional, intellectual, and aesthetic satisfaction that the arts can provide. Indeed, in the 1960s, few Americans living outside the coastal cities had access to live professional performing arts experiences, and arts advocates urged that that situation be remedied.

How times have changed! Thanks in part to these two reports and to the exponential growth of both public arts agencies and arts philanthropy during the 1950s, 1960s, and 1970s, the live, nonprofit professional performing arts grew and prospered along with the economy during the ensuing 35 years. Simultaneously, the world of commercial culture experienced explosive growth as new media—cable television, videotape, and compact discs—joined the film and broadcasting industries in distributing cultural products. Today American life is saturated with arts and cultural activity, and American commercial culture is a powerful—some think, too powerful—presence internationally. Now we are in the throes of yet another technological change, the rapid expansion of digital technologies for the creation and distribution of culture, with unpredictable consequences for the future of the live performing arts.

Broad social changes also expose the vulnerability beneath the apparent robustness of the performing arts. Although the United States maintains its status as the world's most advanced industrial society, we are less optimistic than in the mid-1960s about the imminent prospects of well-being for all our citizens, and we struggle to find solutions to an increasingly complex array of thorny social problems. The arts, only one of many public goods, must compete for both financial resources and the public's attention with an ever-increasing array of other social needs. Furthermore, now that the post–cold war era is more than a decade old, it has become clear that the arts no longer serve as a symbol of national identity and of the freedom and diversity of ideas that underpinned the federal investment in the arts during much of the second half of the 20th century. In addition, the rapid diversification of the nation's populace has both enriched and fragmented our cultural landscape. The nonprofit arts, particularly the performing arts, once again face the possibility of insufficient resources, a threat that makes their future uncertain.

We commissioned this report on the cusp of the 21st century to provide policymakers, arts funders, and the performing arts community with concrete knowledge about the status of the performing arts in this changing environment, and to give ourselves some guidance about how we might work together to respond to the new financial and policy challenges. One of the report's many contributions is its creation of a matrix describing the characteristics of the performing arts system. In this matrix, artists, audiences, organizations, and financing of the performing arts are considered across three domains of activity: the commercial, professional nonprofit, and "volunteer" sectors (the last consisting of a combination of amateur or avocational activities and very-low-budget or grassroots professional activities supported by free or heavily discounted services). RAND has based its findings on often limited existing data about the performing arts. Even so, this methodology yields a more comprehensive picture of the state of the performing arts in the United States than has previously been available.

Although the report provides a clearer understanding and analysis of existing information about the performing arts in the United States, it reveals more starkly than before the continuing lack of reliable data. Two gaps are especially notable: First is the almost complete absence of detailed information about the volunteer sector, making this very large arena of activity virtually invisible to policymakers, philanthropies, and the media. Second is the lack of hard data on the effect of digital technologies and the Internet on the performing arts.

Some of the findings of this study will verify perceptions among performing artists, managers and funders about current challenges and prospects for the future. It will not surprise those involved in the performing arts, for example, that financial pressures are greatest on midsized nonprofit organizations. Other findings and observations in the report may come as a surprise. Many may be struck by the sheer number of Americans who engage in some kind of avocational arts practice. The realignment of performing arts organizations, from a system defined by the two poles of nonprofit and for-profit activity to one defined by organizational size, provides another surprise. And the finding that the largest nonprofit performing arts organizations select programming, undertake marketing activities, and operate in many ways that are indistinguishable from commercial entertainment corporations is certain to spark debate.

RAND's most important recommendation is that those concerned about the well-being of the performing arts in the United States focus greater attention on the public purposes and benefits of the arts and bring greater resources to bear on stimulating demand for the arts. Because public and philanthropic arts policy over the past half-century has concentrated more on building and strengthening the supply of artists, organizations, and productions than on stimulating the public's demand for the arts, this recommendation points toward a profound policy shift.

No doubt these findings and recommendations will be discussed, critiqued, and modified in the future. We hope that this study will make a substantive contribution to that policy debate and will thereby help ensure a strong and confident future for the performing arts in America.

Marian A. Godfrey
Stephen Urice

The Pew Charitable Trusts
July 2001

America's cultural life at the beginning of the 21st century is evolving and diversifying in complex ways. This report is an attempt to describe a part of that evolution: the world of the performing arts. It employs a system-wide perspective by examining the full range of performing arts disciplines (theater, opera, dance, and music) in both their live and recorded forms. Because this study is an ambitious undertaking in a field where critical data are often missing, it includes an assessment of the state of information on the performing arts and defines important concepts needed to analyze them.

This work was supported by The Pew Charitable Trusts as part of its cultural initiative, "Optimizing America's Cultural Resources." One of the objectives of this program is to help build research capability in the arts that will foster discussion and communication among cultural leaders, policymakers, journalists, artists, the philanthropic funding community, and the American public. We hope this report not only provides useful information about broad developments in the performing arts, but also articulates a framework for analyzing and interpreting the implications of these developments.

CONTENTS

Foreword iii

Preface vii

Figures xiii

Tables xv

Summary xvii

Acknowledgments xxvii

Chapter One
INTRODUCTION 1
Approach 2
Organization of the Report 4

Chapter Two
CONCEPTUAL FRAMEWORK 5
What Are the Performing Arts? 5
Key Dimensions of the Performing Arts System 6
Art Form 7
Market Sector 7
Functional Components 9

Chapter Three
HISTORICAL BACKGROUND 11
A New Model of Organization 11
New Methods of Funding 13
Greater Diversity and Participation 14
A Realignment in the Performing Arts System 15

Chapter Four
AUDIENCES FOR THE PERFORMING ARTS 17
Key Concepts 17
Levels of Participation 18

Characteristics of Participants   19
Factors That Influence Participation   19
Sources of Data   19
Current Patterns of Demand   20
Levels of Participation   20
Who Participates?   22
Why Do They Participate?   25
Key Trends   28
More Attendees but Stable Rates of Attendance   28
Growing Participation Through the Media   31
Consumer Desire for Greater Flexibility   33
Future Issues   33
Demographic Changes   33
Economic Changes   34
The Role of Technology   35

Chapter Five
ARTISTS: CREATORS AND PERFORMERS   37
Key Concepts   38
Data Sources   39
Current Picture   40
Artists' Characteristics   40
Employment   41
Career Dynamics   43
Key Trends   45
Increasing Prominence of Superstars   45
More Artists, Fewer Job Opportunities   46
Intellectual Property Questions Created by New Technologies   48
Future Issues   48

Chapter Six
CHARACTERISTICS OF PERFORMING ARTS
ORGANIZATIONS   51
Key Concepts   52
Sources of Data   56
Number of Organizations and Their Disciplines   56
Real Output   58
Programming   59
Current Picture   60
The Live Performing Arts   60
The Recorded Performing Arts   67
Key Trends   70
The Average Nonprofit Performing Group Is Getting Smaller; the
Average For-Profit Is Getting Bigger   70

Patterns of Growth Differ by Sector and Discipline 71
Nonprofit Performing Arts Venues Are Proliferating 73
Future Issues. 74
Dynamism of Small, Volunteer-Sector Performers 75
Rapid Growth of the Performing Arts Infrastructure 75
Increasing Concentration of the Recorded Arts 75
Impact of the Internet 76

Chapter Seven
FINANCIAL SITUATION OF PERFORMING ARTS
ORGANIZATIONS 77
Key Concepts 78
Data Sources 80
Current Picture 82
The Earnings Gap Is Still Substantial 82
Contributed Income Has Been Making Up the Difference 83
Key Trends 85
Direct Public Funding Declined Through Most of the 1990s 85
Private Contributions Have Been Climbing, but Funding
Practices Are Changing 87
Earned Income Has Been Stable and Costs Do Not Appear to Be
Rising 89
Nonprofit Performing Groups Remain Under Financial Pressure . . . 90
For-Profit Firms Also Face Increasing Financial Pressures 91
Organizations Are Using Multiple Strategies to Deal with Financial
Pressures 92
Future Issues. 103
Government Support 103
Private Philanthropy 104
Diversification of Income Sources 104
Emphasis on Earned Income 105

Chapter Eight
WHERE ARE THE PERFORMING ARTS HEADED? 107
A Vision of the Future 107
Implications for the Performing Arts 110
Considerations for Policy 114
Recommendations for Future Research 120

Bibliography 125

FIGURES

2.1. Classification of the Arts 7

4.1. Rates of Participation in the Arts, by Discipline 23

4.2. Education as a Correlate of Attendance 24

4.3. Explaining Participation Preferences 27

4.4. Gains in Attendance by Discipline, 1982–1997 28

4.5. Composition of Change in Attendance by Discipline, 1982–1997 30

4.6. Growth of Participation in the Arts Through the Media, 1982–1997 31

5.1. Proportion of All Artists Who Are Performing Artists 41

5.2. Growth in the Number of Professional Artists, 1970–1990 46

6.1. Organizational Structure of the Professional Performing Arts Delivery System 52

6.2. Proportion of Nonprofit and For-Profit Performing Companies by Discipline, 1997 61

6.3. Percentage of Nonprofit and For-Profit Performing Groups Within Revenue Classes, 1997 62

6.4. Arts Presenters' Programming Activity by Discipline, 1993 67

6.5. Changes in the Number and Revenue Size of Performing Organizations, 1982–1997 71

6.6. Annual Increases in Numbers of Performing Organizations by Discipline, 1982–1997 72

6.7. Annual Change in Average Total Revenues for Performing Groups by Discipline, 1982–1997 73

6.8. Establishment of Performing Venues by Decade,
      as of 1993 74

7.1. Average Earnings Gap for Nonprofit Performing Groups,
      1997 82

7.2. Earned Income as a Percentage of Total Revenue, 1997 83

7.3. Sources of Revenue for Nonprofit Performing Arts
      Organizations, 1997 84

7.4. Government Funding for the Arts, 1970–1999 85

7.5. Fiscal Year 2000 Budgets and Appropriations per Capita for
      Arts Agencies at Three Levels of Government 87

7.6. Philanthropic Giving to the Arts, 1977–1997 88

7.7. Earned Income as Percentage of Total Revenues,
      1977–1997 89

7.8. Annual Percentage Changes in Average Real Expenditures
      of Nonprofit Performing Arts Companies, 1987–1997 90

7.9. Distribution of Performances for Broadway Plays, 1927–28
      and 1959–60 Seasons 98

TABLES

4.1. Annual Participation Rates for Various Leisure-Time
Activities 21

5.1. Employment Characteristics of Performing Artists
Compared with Other Professions 42

6.1. Total Revenues and Percentage of Revenues Held by the 4
Largest and the 20 Largest Performing Companies, 1997 63

6.2. Membership of APAP by Category of Presenting
Organization, 1993 66

6.3. Numbers of Recorded Arts Organizations by Activity, 1997 68

6.4. Percentage of Receipts by Largest Recorded Performing Arts
Firms, 1997 69

Media coverage of the performing arts in America paints a contradictory picture. On the one hand, the arts appear to be booming: the number of organizations offering live performances continues to grow, Broadway plays and live opera performances are bringing in record audiences, and the demand for commercial recordings is stronger than ever. Other stories, however, focus on theater groups, symphony orchestras, and dance companies that are cutting costs or closing their doors because they are unable to attract the audiences and contributions needed to meet their expenses. How can these stories be reconciled? What are the overall trends affecting the performing arts in the last few decades, and what do they imply about the future of arts in America?

In this report, we address these questions by examining key trends in the performing arts since the 1970s. This study is the first of its kind to provide a comprehensive overview of the performing arts. It synthesizes available data on theater, opera, dance, and music, in both their live and recorded forms. Although most of the data are about the nonprofit performing arts—and those data have serious limitations—we also analyze the commercial performing arts (for example, the recording industry and Broadway theater) as well as the volunteer sector, which consists of arts activities that are carried out primarily by amateur and small community-oriented nonprofit groups. After a brief historical background, we focus on trends affecting four aspects of the arts— audiences, artists, arts organizations, and financing—both in the aggregate and, where the data allow, by discipline and sector. Because data limitations often pose limits on the analysis, we also assess the usefulness of available data in each of these areas.

From this broad perspective, we see evidence of a fundamental shift in the structure of the performing arts system. While the commercial recorded and broadcast performing arts industry is growing more and more concentrated globally, live performances are proliferating at the local level, typically in very small organizations with low operating budgets and a mix of paid and unpaid performers and staff. At the same time, a few very large nonprofit as well as commercial organizations are growing larger and staging more elaborate productions. Midsized nonprofit organizations, on the other hand, are facing the greatest difficulty in attracting enough of the public to cover their costs. Many of these organizations are likely to disappear.

HISTORICAL BACKGROUND

In the 19th century, the performing arts were provided to the American public exclusively by commercial or amateur artists and organizations. Most performances were staged in large cities or by touring groups in smaller towns and outlying areas by for-profit enterprises managed by individual owners, who made little distinction between high and popular arts in terms of either programming or audiences. By the turn of the century, these organizations had begun to disappear in the face of new technologies—first recorded music, then film, radio, and ultimately television. The diversion of a large base of customers away from the live proprietary arts began the first major transformation of the performing arts world: presentation of the live high arts within a new nonprofit sector, with the more popular arts, both live and recorded, falling largely into the commercial sector.

By mid-century, the live professional performing arts were being provided primarily by a few elite nonprofit arts institutions centered in major metropolitan areas and supported by a handful of major patrons of the arts. But in the late 1950s and early 1960s, changes in the structure of financial support for the arts—particularly the new financing technique of leveraged funding initiated by the Ford Foundation—stimulated massive growth in the number and diversity of arts funders. This in turn led to a period of unprecedented expansion and geographic dispersion of nonprofit arts organizations across the country.

Over the past two decades, however, while expansion has continued, there are signs that growth from leveraged funding may not be sustainable. Further, the live performing arts appear to be losing out as the American public increasingly chooses to experience the performing arts through recorded and broadcast media. The strategies that both nonprofit and for-profit performing arts organizations are adopting as a result of these developments are changing the shape of the entire performing arts system, with implications for what will be performed and how it will be delivered in the future.

AUDIENCES

The number of Americans attending live performances and purchasing recorded performances has been growing consistently over the years. The most dramatic growth has been in the market for the non-live arts, both recorded and broadcast performances. The popularity of media delivery can be attributed to several factors: the increasing quality of electronically reproduced substitutes for live performances, the rising direct and indirect costs of attending a live performance, and an increasing preference among Americans for home-based leisure activities.

But Americans have also been attending more live performances of all kinds. The most reliable data on attendance show very slight increases in attendance over the 10 years from 1982 to 1992. More recent data from 1997—although less reliable than the earlier data—show the number of people attending live performances going up by 4 percent (opera) to 16 percent (musicals) between 1992 and 1997. Most of the growth in attendance since 1982 is the result of population growth and increasing education levels, not an increase in the percentage of the population that engages in the arts. This distinction is important because slower population growth and shifts in the composition of the population—both of which are expected in the future—may weaken attendance levels.

Several other sociodemographic trends are likely to further dampen demand for live performances in the future. Although education levels are expected to rise—a trend that should create more demand for the arts—Americans are placing an increasing premium on flexibility in their leisure activities. They favor art experiences and other leisure activities that allow them to choose what they want to do, when and where they want to do it. (This preference helps to explain record levels of attendance at art museums.) Additionally, baby boomers will gradually be replaced by a younger generation that appears less inclined to attend live performances and is more comfortable with entertainment provided through the Internet and other emerging technologies. The uncertain status of arts education in public schools may also be a factor in reducing demand for the arts, although little research has been conducted in this area.

ARTISTS

Overall, three broad trends characterize the population of artists. First, their numbers have been growing dramatically. The prodigious increase in both nonprofit and commercial arts organizations between 1970 and 1990 led to a doubling in the number of self-proclaimed professional artists over that period to 1.6 million, about 261,000 of whom are performing artists. The number of amateur performing artists—those who pursue their craft as an avocation with no expectation of being paid for it—is also increasing and they are estimated to outnumber professionals by a factor of 20 or 30 to 1.

Second, performing artists continue to dedicate themselves to their art despite the fact that their pay and job security have scarcely improved since the 1970s.

Performing artists, on average, earn considerably less, work fewer weeks a year, and face higher unemployment than other professionals with comparable education levels. The median annual salary of professional and technical workers in 1989, for example, was 10 percent higher than the median salary of professional actors and directors, and more than twice as high as the median salaries of musicians, composers, and dancers. Moreover, these salary figures for artists include non-arts income from the part-time jobs that artists, unlike other professional workers, tend to hold when they are unable to find work in their chosen profession.

Third, the presence of superstars continues to tilt the arts toward a select few performers. Technological advances have helped magnify small differences in talent and diffuse that information, while marketing efforts have focused increasingly on certain artists as "the best." These developments tend to coalesce demand around a very few stars and drive their wages above everyone else's in the field. Like professional athletes, few performing artists make it to the top, but many are inspired by stories of those who do. Potentially, new technologies such as the Internet could give artists more control over their futures by allowing them to market themselves directly to audiences. But it seems more likely that the importance of critics and marketers will increase, not decrease, in an Internet-driven entertainment world.

PERFORMING ARTS ORGANIZATIONS

The number of nonprofit performing arts organizations increased by over 80 percent between 1982 and 1997, whereas the number of commercial performing arts organizations increased by over 40 percent. At the same time, real revenues for the average nonprofit performing group have declined in all disciplines except opera, suggesting that most of the new nonprofit organizations are small. These small companies—especially those with annual revenues under $100,000—tend to emphasize local participation and rely heavily on unpaid labor.

Performing arts venues (where performances take place) have been constructed at a rapid pace in the past 30 years. According to 1993 data collected by the Association of Performing Arts Presenters, over one-third of all its member establishments were built between 1980 and 1993. Most of these organizations are tax-exempt, and many receive strong financial support from local governments. Such expansion of the arts infrastructure probably reflects the growing emphasis on the economic benefits of the arts on the part of major financers and local and state governments. Many theaters, symphony halls, and all-purpose performing arts centers, for example, are financed by community development block grants. It is not clear, however, who will use these facilities and whether their day-to-day operations will be affordable to many performing groups.

In contrast to the live performing arts, commercial organizations in the recording and broadcasting industries have been consolidating. These two industries are now among the most concentrated in the United States, and they are increasingly organized on a global scale.

FINANCES

The revenues of America's nonprofit arts organizations fall into three main categories: earned income (ticket sales, other business activities, and investment income), philanthropic contributions (from individuals, foundations, and businesses), and direct government subsidies. In the 20 years between 1977 and 1997, as total average annual revenues for performing arts organizations rose steadily, the percentage received from earned income, contributions, and government remained remarkably steady. Despite anecdotes about empty seats at live performances, aggregate data on earned income for nonprofit performing groups do not show a clear downward trend in any of the art forms. The average percentage of total revenues that are earned varies by discipline, with dance companies at the low end with about 30 percent and theater groups at the high end with about 60 percent. In the aggregate, performing groups are about as dependent upon the market as they have been in the past, despite intensive efforts at marketing and audience development, and despite sharp rises in the cost of tickets. (Average ticket prices for orchestras, for example, increased by 70 percent between 1985 and 1995.)

On average, performing arts organizations receive only 5 percent of their revenues from government funding, according to 1997 data, and the level of government subsidy has trended downward until recently. The main source of the decline has been an almost 50 percent decrease in federal funding since the early 1990s, but that decrease has been moderated by an increase in state and local appropriations. The result has been a shift in government funding from the federal to the state and increasingly the local level, with implications for the average size of grants, the characteristics of grant recipients, and the programming decisions of those recipients. In particular, state and local governments tend to focus less on the arts per se and more on the social and economic benefits to local communities in awarding grants.

In contrast, private contributions from individuals, corporations, and foundations increased steadily from 1977 to 1997. Although contributions from individuals increased more than did any other single source of giving, particularly from 1992 to 1997, there is evidence that this increase has come in the form of more smaller donations that require higher development costs. Funding from corporations has also been growing, but corporate donors are increasingly providing support for targeted purposes rather than giving unrestricted grants that allow organizations more flexibility in using these resources.

Because systematic data are not available on artistic output—such as the number of productions, performances, or admissions tickets sold—trends in real expenses averaged across organizations are difficult to interpret. It is impossible to know, for example, whether the 2.2 percent annual increase in opera companies' expenditures between 1987 and 1997 is due to increased costs per production or an increased number of productions per season. Similarly, the 2.8 percent decline in symphony orchestras' annual expenditures over the same period could reflect greater efficiencies or a cutback on the length of their seasons.

In fact, a good deal of case-study evidence suggests that performing arts organizations are using multiple strategies to deal with financial demands in an increasingly competitive leisure market. The authors describe some of the strategies for cutting costs, developing revenues, and financing performances that various organizations are pursuing, and point out that the size of an organization's budget will often determine which strategies will be most effective. In an effort to increase their revenues, for example, large nonprofits rely more on star-studded blockbuster productions, midsized organizations on "warhorse" programming (traditional works loved by general audiences), and small commercial, nonprofit, and especially volunteer organizations more on niche markets. Many large nonprofits have also adopted for-profit business models in order to stabilize revenues: as their productions grow larger and more elaborate, and the celebrity artists they feature more expensive, many large nonprofits are turning to the same revenue-enhancing and financing techniques that have long been popular among for-profit firms, such as merchandising spin-off products and collaborating with financial partners in productions or facility construction.

A VISION OF THE FUTURE

If trends observed in the past 20 years continue, a fundamental shift in the performing arts system will take place. Instead of a sharp demarcation between a nonprofit sector producing the live high arts and a for-profit sector producing mass entertainment, major divisions in the future will be along the lines of big versus small arts organizations, or firms that cater to broad versus niche markets.

Big organizations—both commercial and nonprofit—will rely increasingly on massive advertising and marketing campaigns promoting celebrity artists to attract large audiences. Although for-profit firms will still focus primarily on the recorded arts (with the notable exception of Broadway), and nonprofits will continue live performances, distinctions between what is "popular art" and what is "high art" will continue to erode as both sets of organizations seek to produce the next blockbuster. And as the rewards of success and the costs of failure climb, these large organizations will seek to minimize their risks by choosing conservative programming and technology-intensive productions designed to appeal to the largest possible audience.

At the other end of the scale, small performing arts organizations will be both more dynamic and more diverse than their larger counterparts. In the commercial sector, small firms will target niche markets within the recorded branches of the performing arts. At times these firms will move into areas such as classical recordings that have been abandoned by larger firms because they do not provide the margins and volume that large firms require. Technological changes such as the Internet and e-commerce will enable small for-profits to provide more adventuresome programming that serves a wider variety of smaller, more specialized markets.

In the nonprofit and volunteer sectors, the growing number of small organizations will have little in common with larger nonprofits in terms of programming, audience demographics, and the professional stature of most of their artists. Small performing arts groups will focus on low-budget, low-tech live productions that rely heavily on volunteer labor. Many will cater to local and specialized markets, particularly ethno-cultural communities and neighborhoods. Others will provide opportunities for hands-on participation for nonprofessional artists in traditional high-arts forms.

The biggest change suggested by these trends relates to the middle tier of nonprofit arts organizations, particularly those opera companies, symphony orchestras, ballet companies, and theater groups located outside of major metropolitan areas. Likely reductions in demand, rising costs, and static or even declining funding streams will force many of these institutions either to become larger and more prestigious—which many will lack the resources to do—or to become smaller and more community-oriented, using local talent to keep costs down and adapting programming to local audiences. Still others will simply close their doors, unable to reconcile conflicts among their various stakeholders.

IMPLICATIONS FOR THE ARTS

What will these trends mean for the vitality of the performing arts in the future? How are they likely to affect the quantity, quality, and availability of the arts, in particular? The vision of the future we describe here suggests that the quantity of performances will increase in some areas and decrease in others, depending on whether they are live or recorded, and whether they involve the high, folk, or popular arts. Professional live performances of the high arts, for example, will be increasingly concentrated in big cities and provided by high-budget nonprofit organizations that can support the cost of top-echelon performers and productions. Touring artists and performing groups will bring the live professional arts to audiences in smaller cities and towns that are not able to sustain top-level performing arts.

The recorded and broadcast performing arts should continue to proliferate and diversify. Advances in production, recording, and distribution technologies will allow Americans to choose among a wider variety of performances and art forms than they do today. Although the Internet's ability to produce sustained profitability remains to be demonstrated, it is already reaching far-flung audiences and creating healthy markets for art forms that have previously been unable to attract economically significant demand. In the future, niche arts markets may be not only possible, but profitable.

Americans will also have increasing access to live performances in their own communities. Small professional nonprofit and for-profit performing groups will be able to build and maintain comparatively small but loyal audiences who value their artistry and are willing to participate both as consumers and patrons of the arts. Small organizations in the volunteer sector will continue to provide low-budget productions of great cultural and artistic diversity performed largely by artists who practice their craft as an avocation.

The effect of future changes on the quality of the arts could be more serious. Several trends are likely to make it more difficult for talented actors, composers, musicians, and dancers to mature artistically. If the polarization of artistic incomes created by the superstar phenomenon continues to grow and the number of both large and midsized arts organizations contracts, young artists will have fewer opportunities to gain experience in their field. Moreover, the pressures on performing arts organizations to earn ever-greater revenues tend to produce programming that appeals to mass audiences in both the large nonprofit and the commercial worlds. As market categories with demonstrated success increasingly govern the selection of what gets performed and recorded, innovation is likely to be discouraged. Even the decentralized distribution system provided by the Internet poses its own obstacles: With so many artists entering the scene, it becomes harder for artists of unusual talent to attract the attention of more than a small circle of admirers.

The effects of change on access to the arts will be mixed, as are the effects on quantity. Although live professional performances will decline in some parts of the country, community-based performances and recorded products will proliferate. Access will most likely hinge on future patterns of demand.

CONSIDERATIONS FOR POLICY

How does our analysis of the performing arts help inform discussions of policy? The critical issue in arts policy is how current trends affect the broader public interest, and this issue has not been given adequate attention by the arts community. Developing a policy-analytic capability for the arts today will require a new framework that is grounded in an understanding of the public interests served by the arts, the roles that government (versus others) could play in promoting those interests, and the strategies that government at every level has at its disposal.

We conclude by discussing each of these aspects of a policy framework and identifying future research areas that would contribute to the development of such a framework. Until recently, the policy debate has been too narrowly focused on supporting the production and performance of the arts—"supply" strategies—rather than stimulating public involvement in the arts—"demand" strategies. A new framework that puts the public benefits of the arts at the center of the discussion will require approaches designed to increase individual exposure, knowledge, and access to the arts. Future research should examine how individual tastes for the arts are formed and how the public and private benefits of the arts can be identified and measured, so that policymakers can explore more diversified and innovative approaches to promoting the arts in American society.

ACKNOWLEDGMENTS

This work could not have been conducted without the encouragement, guidance, and assistance of many people. We would like to give particular thanks to Marian Godfrey, Stephen Urice, and Shelley Feist of the Culture Program at The Pew Charitable Trusts for their support and advice throughout the research process. We are also indebted to the arts researchers and cultural leaders who offered us assistance in gathering information on the arts and who attended seminar presentations of this work, including Kelly Barsdate, Elizabeth Boris, Tom Bradshaw, Ben Cameron, Joan Channick, Randy Cohen, Doug DeNatale, Paul DiMaggio, Ann Gray, Mark Hager, Frank Hodsoll, Maria Rosario Jackson, Joan Jeffri, William Luksetich, Jack McCauliffe, Tom Pollak, J. Mark Schuster, Joan Shigekawa, Holly Sidford, Andras Szanto, James Allen Smith, Steven Tepper, Andrew Tyndall, and Margaret Wyszomirski. Many of these individuals also offered thoughtful comments on earlier drafts of this report.

We also wish to thank the national arts service organizations for explaining their data collection efforts to us and, where feasible, providing us with data. In particular we wish to thank Charles Olton, Jack McAuliffe, and Jan Wilson of the American Symphony Orchestra League; John Munger of Dance/USA; John Church, Betsy Cecchetti, and Stacey March of OPERA America; and Ben Cameron, Joan Channick, Chris Shuff, and Collette Carter of Theater Communications Group. Roland Kushner provided tremendous assistance in gathering, compiling, and assessing these data.

Special thanks go to David Throsby of Macquarie University, Sydney, Australia, and our RAND colleague, C. R. Neu. Their thoughtful reviews occasioned many changes that improved the clarity and accuracy of the report. And last but not least, we would like to thank Renee Almassizadeh, Aimee Bower, Phil Devin, Lisa Jones, Tessa Kaganoff, Elizabeth Ondaatje, Lauren Sager, Roberta

Shanman, and Lilah Shapiro for research support; and Lisa Lewis, Miriam Polon, David Bolhuis, and Eileen La Russo for production support.

The opinions expressed in this report are those of the authors and do not necessarily reflect the views of The Pew Charitable Trusts.

Chapter One

INTRODUCTION

The best of times or the worst of times? Charles Dickens' famous aphorism aptly describes the polarization of observers of American arts and culture at the dawn of the 21st century. To some, "mid-to-late twentieth century Western culture . . . will go down in history as a fabulously creative and fertile epoch" in which "growth of the market has liberated artists, not only from the patron, but also from the potential tyranny of mainstream market taste" (Cowen, 1998, p. 8). To others, "high art in America is dying" because Americans do not properly appreciate "the concept of a culture driven by art and inspiration rather than by the cash register" (Brustein, 1992, 1995). At the heart of this debate are profound differences of opinion about the changes in the arts that have taken place over the last two to three decades, particularly the increasing role of the marketplace in the delivery of the arts.

What is the nature of these changes, especially in the performing arts? On one hand, there is ample evidence that this is a period of extraordinary growth in American arts activity, popular involvement, and international influence. On the other, newspapers regularly report that theaters, symphonies, and dance groups are struggling financially, unable to attract the audiences and contributions they need to meet their costs. How can these stories be reconciled? What do the data tell us about key trends: attendance at live performances, consumption of recorded and broadcast performances, the supply and remuneration of artists and performers, funding for the arts, and the financial condition of organizations, both nonprofit and for-profit? Are some artistic disciplines and forms of arts consumption growing while others are declining? And what do these trends suggest about the future of the performing arts?

The central purpose of this study is to address these questions. Using the data and analysis available, we describe the performing arts today with an emphasis on the forces of change that are likely to shape the performing arts in the future. We look at the entire system of the performing arts—including the nonprofit sector, the commercial market, and what we choose to call the volunteer sector, by which we mean arts activities that are carried out primarily by avocational and small community-oriented nonprofit groups—in order to identify how activities across the various parts of the system may be related. Such a systems approach is an important step in the evolution of the field of cultural policy analysis. We must understand the boundaries of the system; the key dimensions along which it can be described; and the trends affecting public involvement in the arts, artists, arts organizations, and financing in all parts of the system before we can identify and assess alternative policies that might be considered in addressing these trends.

The main difficulty in conducting such an analysis is that the data needed to answer such questions with confidence often do not exist. On the commercial side, for example, the recording industry releases almost no data on the costs of its operations. Nor can we determine what the total annual revenues are from recorded music or from music and opera videos. Information on the nonprofit arts is much more plentiful, but the data often lack the adequate differentiation and systematic collection over time that are needed to analyze artistic products and the audiences for different art forms. Because the data are fragmentary and incomplete, the literature on the art world suffers from several weaknesses: academic studies tend to be narrowly focused on areas where the data are plentiful; commentary for broader audiences tends to take on larger issues but usually provides only anecdotal evidence for support; and the field in general lacks a systematic framework for analyzing the data that do exist.

APPROACH

In view of these difficulties, we approached our task from the broadest possible perspective. We wanted to understand how existing information describes the world of the performing arts in the United States, where the gaps in information are, and how trends in one part of the performing arts might be influencing trends in other parts of the system.

We began with a literature review that included all datasets on the arts and all policy-relevant research studies over the last 20 years—not only about the performing arts but about the visual arts, literary arts, and media arts as well.[1] Examining information sources on such a wide range of topics on the arts helped us create a framework with which to describe and analyze different parts of the performing arts system (see Chapter Two).

The portrait of the performing arts in this report is largely a work of synthesis. Although we did some new empirical analysis of the data and drew conclusions

---

[1] The data sources and research studies cited in this report are limited to the performing arts. The compendium of sources including the performing, visual, literary, and media arts will be released separately.

from this analysis that are not widely recognized, our main purpose was to systematize and synthesize work that has already been done on the arts. Looking across artistic disciplines, market sectors, and the different ways performances are experienced (live, recorded, broadcast), we have connected many disparate pieces of information and analysis. In the process, we looked for common patterns among distinct studies, links among trends in the data from different parts of the system, and relationships between these trends and the broad context of sociodemographic, economic, and technological change that influence individual attitudes toward the arts, the way Americans choose to spend their leisure time, and the ways artistic performances are delivered to the public. We acknowledge that there is a good deal of intuition and personal judgment in such a synthesis. But the breadth of our approach has allowed us to identify forces of change in the performing arts that would not have been visible through a narrower lens.

In undertaking this research, we made no initial assumptions about the proper role of government in the arts or about the value of one kind of artistic expression or experience over another. We have tried to avoid any type of advocacy for the arts in order to conduct the kind of impartial empirical analysis that forms the basis of sound policy. Our main purpose has been to improve understanding of the recent changes in the support structure for the performing arts and what they may mean for the future of the arts. Although we highlight several issues that we believe merit future policy consideration, we do not assess specific policy options for the arts.

Our research offers evidence of a fundamental shift in the structure of the live performing arts in the future. Specifically, we predict that the number of organizations supplying live performances of theater, music, opera, and dance will contract at the professional level and expand at the community level. Organizations that produce live professional performances face particular problems in many small and midsized cities across the country and could become increasingly concentrated in large metropolitan areas and important regional centers that can support high-budget nonprofit organizations with top-echelon performers and productions. For many Americans, access to this level of performing art will depend on touring productions. At the same time, Americans will have greater access to small, low-budget productions of great cultural and artistic diversity performed largely by amateur artists (and professionals willing to perform for little or no pay) in their own communities. Also, as is true today, Americans will increasingly choose to experience the performing arts not through live performances but through recordings and broadcast media, the quality of which will continue to improve.

This future is far from certain, and some areas of the country may make a sustained commitment to maintaining their nonprofit cultural institutions. Many smaller and midsized cities, for example, look with understandable civic pride upon their local performing-arts organizations as important community assets and have increased their financial support accordingly. Nevertheless, taken together, the trends discussed in this report point to a growing polarization in the delivery of both live and recorded arts into very large and small organizations. The implications of such a development for the vitality of the performing arts—and for the public good—should become part of the broader discussion of arts policy in America.

ORGANIZATION OF THE REPORT

The next chapter describes the conceptual framework for our analysis. Chapter Three offers a brief history of the way in which the performing arts have been provided to the public from the late 19th century to the present, with emphasis on the changing role of the marketplace in the arts. The next four chapters provide our analysis of the audiences and other consumers of the performing arts (Chapter Four), performing artists (Chapter Five), the characteristics of performing arts organizations (Chapter Six), and the financial situation of those organizations (Chapter Seven). Each of these chapters is structured in the same way. First, we describe the key concepts that define any inquiry into the subject. For example, the chapter on audiences describes the various ways in which people become involved in the arts, how that involvement can be measured over time, and how changes in those measurements can be interpreted. Second, we describe the kind of data needed to analyze the subject adequately, and we assess the quality of the data that exist. Finally, we present our analysis, starting with a description of the current state of affairs—such as the sociodemographic characteristics of today's audiences—and moving to a description of the main trends over the last 15 to 20 years and what they suggest for the future.

The final chapter synthesizes these trends, describes their implications for the future, and suggests the kinds of questions they pose for public policy in the arts. It also identifies where there are major gaps in our understanding of the performing arts and suggests corresponding priorities for future research.

Chapter Two

CONCEPTUAL FRAMEWORK

We viewed this study as an opportunity to help build the foundation for policy analysis in the arts. Our approach was to follow a familiar sequence of steps required for policy analysis: (1) define the population of interest, (2) identify a key set of analytical dimensions along which to describe that population, (3) use those dimensions to describe the current state of affairs and trends, (4) identify the dynamics behind those trends, (5) examine the range of policies that can affect those trends, and (6) evaluate the costs and benefits of those policy options. The last two activities are commonly recognized as the central tasks of policy analysis. They cannot be performed, however, without first defining and describing the subject area being analyzed, both as it is now and as it has been changing. This task has yet to be accomplished for the arts.

For that reason, this analysis focuses on the early steps of the process, steps 1 through 4, and offers a brief discussion of policy implications that arise from that analysis (step 5). In this chapter, we describe the first two steps of the process: how we defined the performing arts and the dimensions we used to analyze them.

WHAT ARE THE PERFORMING ARTS?

The population of interest in this study was the entire system of production and consumption of the performing arts. By the performing arts we mean theater, music, opera, and dance, from the traditional "high arts" to the popular arts, including live arts performed in all venues and non-live arts through all forms of mass media: CDs and other recordings, radio, video, television, and the Internet. We have excluded the genre of film from our scope.[1]

---

[1]A related RAND study supported by the Rockefeller Foundation is examining the rise of the media arts, including independent film. That work is forthcoming.

We refer to the "high," "popular," and "folk" arts in our analysis to describe parts of the performing arts market that are relatively distinct. Although we recognize that these distinctions are easier to draw in broad strokes than in all their details, they do reflect important differences in how the performing arts are produced and distributed. The high arts are traditional art forms such as ballet and symphonic music. The popular arts consist of art forms such as rock and roll music or musical theater that have attracted mass audiences in the commercial marketplace. The folk arts range from gospel music to Khmer classical dance and represent the traditional art and culture of the diverse ethnic communities within the United States. Many live folk arts performances are produced by amateur (i.e., unpaid) artists and small nonprofit performing groups in the volunteer sector.

We do not mean to suggest by these terms, however, that certain art forms or types of participation are inherently more worthy than others. Although the data on amateur activity are scanty and largely anecdotal because it tends to take place outside official organizations or in non-arts organizations such as schools and churches, such activity represents an extremely important part of the performing arts in America today. As the following description of our conceptual framework suggests, the different environments for the performing arts—the nonprofit, commercial, and volunteer sectors—need to be clearly delineated in order to identify how each is evolving.

KEY DIMENSIONS OF THE PERFORMING ARTS SYSTEM

How is such a vast network of related activity to be described? We needed a conceptual framework—a kind of multidimensional map—that could provide a structure for describing and analyzing all aspects of the performing arts system and could help us classify all the information sources on the performing arts into a coherent system. One grid on that map, of course, had to be the art form itself. The performing arts consist of multiple disciplines, each of which has different modes of production and involves different types of organizations. Another grid on the map is the one mentioned above: the sector of the economy in which the art is performed and produced. The same work of art can be produced in different sectors of the market—through nonprofit, commercial, or volunteer means—in a variety of forms. The third dimension, which has the richest potential for systems analysis, defines the key players in the process of creating the art and delivering it to audiences. These are audiences, artists, arts organizations, and funders of the arts. All of these dimensions must be analyzed to get a full picture of the performing arts system.

Art Form

As illustrated in Figure 2.1, art forms can be classified into four main categories: the performing arts, the media arts, the visual arts, and the literary arts.[2] Each of these is further subdivided. Within the performing arts, for example, we draw distinctions among theater, dance, music, and opera. In theory, each of these different disciplines can be divided further into a great number of subdisciplines, such as ballet, folk dancing, modern dance, and tap dancing, although very little data exist at this level of detail.

Market Sector

The second dimension of our framework consists of the three market sectors in which the arts are performed and produced: the nonprofit sector, the com-

RAND *MR1367-2.1*

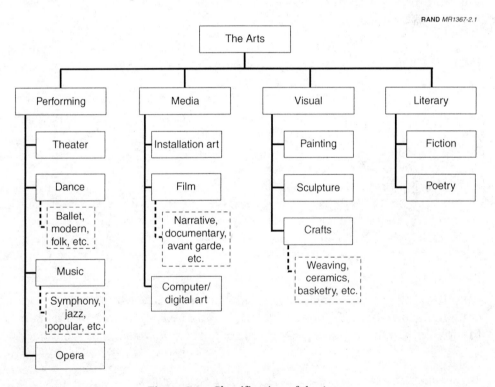

Figure 2.1—Classification of the Arts

---

[2]The subdisciplines illustrated in Figure 2.1 are representative. We do not attempt to list all possible subdisciplines for all the major art forms here. Other classification systems are also possible—for example, Balfe and Peters (2000) use a different classification scheme that includes design and architecture as major categories.

mercial sector, and the volunteer sector. The nonprofit sector consists entirely of arts organizations that have filed for formal nonprofit status under Section 501(c)(3) of the Internal Revenue Code. Although these organizations benefit greatly from contributions of volunteer and subsidized labor, they also depend heavily on philanthropic contributions, or "unearned" income, as well as on earnings from ticket receipts and other sources. In contrast to the profits that drive commercial organizations, nonprofit institutions are "mission-driven," although the missions they pursue are diverse. Examples include Arena Stage in Washington D.C. and the Los Angeles Philharmonic.

Commercial organizations pay taxes, rely solely on the market for financial solvency, and define success in terms of market profitability. While examples range from Disney and Atlantic Records to Broadway theater and jazz nightclubs, most for-profit performing arts organizations are involved in the production and distribution of recorded artistic products rather than live performances.

Finally, the volunteer sector encompasses activities carried out by avocational groups such as church choirs, folk-art groups, and local rock bands, as well as by small nonprofit organizations that may have been formally incorporated as tax-exempt organizations.[3] In contrast to the nonprofit sector, volunteer sector groups rely more on volunteer labor than on monetary contributions to survive; they also tend to give more importance to enlisting and encouraging participation from particular geographic, ethnic, or cultural communities. In fact, this objective is often their primary mission. An example is the Santa Monica Symphony Orchestra, an organization whose nucleus is made up of volunteer musicians. The Santa Monica Symphony does not charge admission to the four concerts it presents in the local civic auditorium each season, and its revenues averaged less than $100,000 per year during the decade of the 1990s. Its primary mission is to serve the residents of Santa Monica and neighboring communities.

Unfortunately, these distinctions among sectors are easier to draw in theory than in practice. Both nonprofit organizations and volunteer groups are likely to combine earnings, contributions, and volunteer labor to support their oper-

---

[3]As we define it, the "volunteer" sector of the arts includes many of the groups and activities typically included in what arts researchers call the "unincorporated" sector, but not all. For example, while this category includes groups that are "small and organized informally, with little economic interchange" as described in Peters and Cherbo (1998, p.116), it does not include the national arts service organizations or arts organizations embedded within larger non-arts nonprofits—both of which are sometimes included in definitions of the unincorporated sector (Peters and Cherbo, 1998; Arthurs and Hodsoll, 1998). More important, our definition of the voluntary sector explicitly includes small organizations that are formally tax-exempt but rely primarily on volunteer labor.

ations, making it difficult to know where to draw the line between "primarily" and "partly" dependent on one revenue source or another. There are also "hybrid" organizations that incorporate features of both the commercial and nonprofit sectors. For example, nonprofit organizations may set up profit-making subsidiaries, or a facility owned by local government may be used by a nonprofit organization and run by volunteer labor. There are almost no data at all on organizations that file under the umbrella of non-arts nonprofit institutions, such as university theaters.

Regardless of how market orientation is defined, it is important to remember that any particular art form can be presented in any sector. Classical music, for example, is offered in live performances by professional symphony orchestras in the nonprofit sector, on CDs produced and sold by commercial firms, and in live performances in the volunteer sector. Although the outcomes are all "high arts" experiences, they may differ in terms of their quality, accessibility, price, and audience. These differences are central to understanding the performing arts today.

Functional Components

By functional components of the performing arts system, we mean the classes of individuals and organizations that serve key functions in the complex process of creating and presenting the arts—artists, audiences, arts organizations, and funders. The process starts with the artist's creation of the work to be performed and ends with the audience's experience of the work. Between the artists and their audiences lies a vast array of organizations and individuals that perform, present, record, and transmit works of art. Supporting these organizations are the individuals, foundations, businesses, and government agencies that offer financial support to nonprofit organizations and, in some cases, invest financially in commercial arts firms. Taken together, all these entities make up the performing arts system.

This classification system is useful because it facilitates analysis of the characteristics of the performing arts industry that make it similar to and different from other industries. Such a breakdown also allows us to examine activities that share the same function and therefore to make comparisons across arts forms and market sectors. For instance, composers and dancers can be both artists and producers of art; for-profit Broadway theaters and nonprofit regional theater houses are both groups of presenters; thus their characteristics can be validly compared.

Using this conceptual framework, we are able to compare arts activities within art form, market sector, and functional domains over time, and to consider how activities across the various dimensions may be related. For example, to answer the question "how has the demand for classical music changed over the past 20 years?" one might look at box office data for nonprofit symphony orchestras for the period 1980 to 2000. Such an approach, however, would miss an important feature of the demand for classical music, which often reaches audiences through recorded media such as tapes and CDs sold on the commercial market or through broadcast media such as radio. Many classical music consumers, after all, enjoy their art through all of these media. Understanding cross-discipline, cross-sector, and cross-function relationships is important for understanding the American arts world at the beginning of the 21st century. Perhaps even more critical, it is essential for accurate forecasting of what is to come. Although we acknowledge that this framework is bound to describe the current structure of the arts better than it does the structure that will evolve in the future, it would be difficult to contemplate that future without using the terms that best describe the present.

Chapter Three

HISTORICAL BACKGROUND

A brief review of the history of the performing arts in the United States provides a useful background for a discussion of more recent trends. This chapter reviews the evolution of the performing arts with a special focus on nonprofit organizations and the unique institutional funding arrangements that have evolved to support them.

In the 19th century, the performing arts were provided to the American public exclusively by commercial or amateur artists and organizations. Unlike Europe during this period, there was essentially no government support of the arts and very little tradition of upper-class patronage. Most performing arts groups were for-profit enterprises managed by individual owners. They made little distinction between the high arts and popular arts in terms of either programming or audiences and performed to mixed crowds that ranged from the working classes to the upper classes. These shows were generally performed in the larger urban centers, or by touring companies of musicians and actors in smaller cities and towns. Apart from such commercial entertainment, a good deal of amateur performance took place in private homes, particularly those of the middle and upper classes. Musical literacy among Americans was relatively high—especially among cultured young women—and performances for friends and family were a popular form of evening entertainment (Butsch, 2000). Folk-art performances were generally restricted to amateur artists and organizations belonging to specific ethnic communities.

A NEW MODEL OF ORGANIZATION

In the first years of the 20th century, however, the commercial touring companies began to decline. According to Baumol and Bowen (1966), there were 327 theater companies at the turn of the century but fewer than 100 in 1915. By the 1930s, only a few were left. The agent of this change was the emergence of the new medium of movies. Many proprietary live performing arts organizations disappeared in the face of the new technologies—first film, then recorded music, radio, and ultimately television. This development marked the beginning of a profound change in the delivery of the performing arts in America. As John Kreidler writes, "Whereas broad-based audiences, comprised of both commoners and educated, well-to-do elites had once attended proprietary productions of Shakespeare, even in small towns and mining camps across the nation, in the twentieth century, the commoners began to gravitate toward the movie houses and other new technologies, leaving only the elite to patronize an assortment of proprietary high art" (Kreidler, 1996, p. 81).

The diversion of a large base of customers away from the live proprietary arts began the first major transformation of the performing arts world: the division of the popular, folk, and high arts that has defined the performing arts in America for the past 100 years. As new recorded forms of arts and entertainment drew audiences away from the live popular arts, the remaining audiences—many of whom had a preference for the high arts—had to accept higher prices to maintain the supply of the art forms they preferred. These increased prices mostly took the form of donations or organizational subsidies rather than user fees. The result was a new model of arts organization: the subsidized nonprofit organization. As Butsch (2000) and DiMaggio (1986) argue, the expanding elite and middle classes also became increasingly unwilling to share their arts experience with the "rowdy and disreputable" working classes. The new organizational model provided them with a means to distinguish themselves through their tastes in art.

The newly emergent nonprofits were supported initially by patrons among the affluent urban elite who were willing to underwrite the establishment of nonprofit institutions devoted to the high arts. Eventually, however, these organizations became too expensive for individuals alone to support and evolved into organizations run by a board of directors or trustees that provided funding and general oversight of the financial health of the institution. By and large, the government played little role in supporting these organizations or the arts more generally. The 1917 adoption of the income tax deduction for individual contributions to educational, health, and cultural organizations, which would later prove a central element of government support for the arts, had little direct impact for at least another decade (Harris, 1995; Hall, 1987).[1] The Depression-era WPA arts programs, which at their peak employed thousands of artists, represent a notable exception to this pattern. But these programs were short-lived and motivated primarily by humanitarian concerns for the unemployed.

---

[1]This policy was extended to corporations in 1936.

NEW METHODS OF FUNDING

The next major transformation occurred in the late 1950s as America, the world's economic and political leader, began to seek comparable stature in the arts. The division of the performing arts world into a live nonprofit high-arts sector, a live or recorded commercial popular sector, and a live unincorporated folk-arts sector was already firmly established. The live high arts were concentrated in major metropolitan areas where they were produced by a few elite institutions that catered to a predominantly affluent white audience. In the late 1950s, the Ford Foundation, under the guidance of W. McNeil Lowry, its vice president for the arts, developed an ambitious scheme for the systematic advancement of the entire arts field. Ford's program had three principal goals: (1) to financially revitalize the major institutions through leveraged investments that required matching support two to four times greater than the amount awarded by the Foundation; (2) to increase access to the high arts through the establishment of new regional institutions that would disperse the high arts beyond the city of New York and other major metropolitan centers, and (3) to professionalize the high arts by establishing conservatories and visual-arts schools to generate a skilled labor force for the increasing number of arts organizations.

The concept of leveraged funding as a tactic for recruiting new donors was perhaps the most significant innovation in the evolution of the arts infrastructure in America, leading to the complex public-private partnerships that characterize the sector today. Before Ford introduced this strategy, very few institutions engaged in arts philanthropy. Following Ford's leadership, however, hundreds of foundations and corporations became active supporters of the arts. The concept, which proved enormously successful for the next 30 years, was that the initial grant would stimulate an ever-expanding base of funding from individuals and institutional funders that would be able to supply the contributed income needed by the nonprofit arts economy to survive.

In 1960, the state of New York took the pioneering step of establishing a State Council for the Arts (Netzer, 1978). The National Endowment for the Arts (NEA) was conceived at about the same time and was inaugurated in 1965. For the first time in U.S. history, the federal government assumed an active role in directly supporting the arts. This reversal of the long-standing opposition to public support for the arts was triggered by a combination of factors, including a desire to demonstrate to the world the value of U.S. culture (as a concomitant to our military and economic power), the acceptance of a broader government role in supporting social goals more generally, the work of arts advocacy groups that lobbied for greater parity with science in the competition for federal support, and widespread belief that the arts and culture were important social assets that could not be sustained in the marketplace (Cherbo and Wyszomirski, 2000; Urice, 1992; Harris, 1995). Baumol and Bowen's influential 1966 analysis of the performing arts, which argued that the live performing arts could never entirely support themselves with earned income, provided an important intellectual foundation for both public and private subsidy of the arts.

Relying on the leveraging strategy initiated by Ford, and motivated by similar goals of increasing access, financial viability, and professionalism, the NEA initiated a program of direct support for artists and nonprofit arts institutions as well as block grants to states. Within 15 years of the formation of the NEA, every state had established an arts agency, which in turn spawned more than 3,000 local arts councils, some of which were organized as units of local government, but most of which became private nonprofit organizations.

GREATER DIVERSITY AND PARTICIPATION

The transformation of the live performing arts sector—primarily the high arts— that was sparked by these developments took several forms: the number, geographic dispersion, and diversity of nonprofit organizations increased several fold; the amount of financial support for the nonprofit arts increased dramatically and came from an increasingly diverse array of sources; and the nonprofit form became the dominant organizational mode in supplying the live high arts to Americans.

This dramatic increase in the supply of nonprofit arts institutions also sparked corresponding increases in arts participation, which were not restricted to attendance but included a resurgence of amateur "hands-on" participation in all of the performing arts (Toffler, 1964). As was true of an earlier era, this surge in participation was supported by the social and economic changes under way in America: increasing prosperity, rising education levels, expanded leisure time, and the arrival of the baby boomers on college campuses were the driving forces behind the emergence of a new arts generation. The availability of new conservatories and college programs devoted to the development of artists swelled the ranks of highly trained creators and performers, some of whom succeeded as professionals but many of whom entered other careers and chose to pursue their art as a leisure activity.

This growing market for the high arts, however, continued to come from a rather narrow band of society—what Toffler (1964) refers to as the "comfort classes." The vast majority of Americans still sought their arts and entertainment from commercial sources, which continued to flourish by providing a growing variety of popular products to expanding national and international markets. Indeed, continued technological advances increased the sophistication and range of products the commercial sector produced and thus the complexity of its delivery system. This expansion in scale and scope increased both the costs and the rewards available in the commercial sector (Vogel, 1998). Folk-art forms also flourished but continued to be practiced by artists and small groups that operated primarily in the volunteer sector.

A REALIGNMENT IN THE PERFORMING ARTS SYSTEM

The next major realignment in the support structure for the arts appears to be taking place now, as a result of changes that have been occurring over the last 10 to 15 years. In the past decade, the leveraged funding paradigm has proved difficult to sustain. Political controversy has reduced federal funding of the arts. The economic recession of the early 1990s also affected private funding patterns as corporate sponsors moved away from unrestricted grants (Cobb, 1996) and foundations became increasingly concerned about the broader benefits of their grants (Renz and Lawrence, 1998). Although individual contributions rose throughout the 1990s, such growth has institutional costs and may not be sustainable.

The stark distinctions that used to exist between the commercial, nonprofit, and volunteer sectors (and the implicit superiority of the nonprofit sector) are also becoming blurred: organizational "hybrids" straddle both sectors and Americans enjoy their arts experiences in many environments both within and outside the marketplace. Rather than being viewed as separate and distinct, these three sectors are increasingly viewed as different elements of a diversified arts environment. Indeed, the different functions these sectors perform are increasingly considered complementary rather than competitive (DiMaggio, 1991). Much attention is being paid to collaboration and the transfer of ideas, functions, and resources—including artists—across sectors. For example, the nonprofit sector is widely perceived as a training ground for artists and a source of research and development (R&D) for the commercial sector by providing a testbed for new works and new performers.

The policy concerns of these different sectors, although still distinguishable, have also begun to overlap in such areas as copyright, intellectual property, trade agreements, and a host of other issues raised by technological developments and consolidations within the communications industry. At the same time, the public debate on arts policy has shifted away from an exclusive focus on public funding for the nonprofit sector and toward a more general concern with the public purposes of the arts and how each sector of the performing arts world promotes those benefits (American Assembly, 1997). In the process, nonprofit arts organizations have given greater priority to a broader set of missions, including more active public participation in all forms of the performing arts.

In keeping with this broader, system-wide perspective toward the arts is a less hierarchical view of their value. It is now more commonly assumed that a pluralistic democratic society should foster artistic activities that reflect the interests and aesthetic tastes of the entire population rather than the cultural leadership of a particular group. Performing in amateur productions in local community settings, for example, is now acknowledged by many to be as important a form of participation as attending a top-quality professional performance.

These changes have their roots in the broad sociodemographic, economic, and political forces that are transforming American society today, such as the growing diversity of the American population, shifts in cultural consumption resulting from changing lifestyles, and a political climate that is promoting smaller government and greater emphasis on privatization and market-oriented approaches for all types of organizations. How are these trends affecting the performing arts today? How are changes in demand and funding patterns affecting arts organizations and with what implications for availability and quality of the arts? The analysis we present in the following chapters will help answer these questions.

Chapter Four

AUDIENCES FOR THE PERFORMING ARTS

The future of the performing arts will be shaped by many factors, but perhaps none is more important than the future structure of demand. As Chapter Three noted, the size and shape of the market for the performing arts has changed over time—reflecting shifts in demand that are stimulated by technological change as well as social, demographic, and economic trends in American society. This chapter focuses on the demand for performing arts today. After a brief discussion of concepts used to define and measure demand and the data available, we address three questions: (1) What does the demand for the performing arts look like now? (2) How has that demand been changing? (3) What issues are these changes likely to pose for the future?

KEY CONCEPTS

Public involvement in the performing arts takes several different forms. Individuals may be involved as producers (at an amateur or professional level), as consumers (by attending a live performance or listening or watching a recorded performance), and as supporters (by donating time or money to arts organizations) (Balfe and Peters, 2000). Although individuals who are involved in one form may also be involved in another, demand for the performing arts is typically gauged by examining patterns of consumption—which are most frequently measured in terms of participation in the performing arts.

Despite the fact that consumption of the performing arts is sometimes equated with attending a performance, people can in fact experience the performing arts in several different ways. Some people may be directly involved in a "hands-on" way by playing an instrument or singing in a choir.[1] For others, consumption means attending a live performance. Still others listen to a

---

[1]We classify "hands-on" involvement here as a form of consumption rather than of production to distinguish between those who play an instrument as a hobby and those who perform in public whether on a paid or volunteer basis.

recording or watch a play on television. These different forms of involvement are important because the empirical literature demonstrates that the level of demand for the performing arts differs, often dramatically, depending upon the art form and how individuals choose to experience it. Indeed, consumption of the performing arts through the media is more prevalent than attendance at live performances, and many more people participate through their attendance than by engaging in the arts in a hands-on manner (NEA, 1998a; Americans for the Arts, 1996).

The empirical literature on the performing arts routinely describes demand patterns in terms of three different elements: the level of participation, the characteristics of participants, and the factors that influence participation.

Levels of Participation

Three different metrics are used to measure levels of participation:

- absolute level of consumption, typically measured in terms of the total amount of participation, e.g., total attendance levels

- rate of participation during a given period, typically reported as a percentage of the population (or subpopulations) who participate

- frequency of participation among those who actually participate, such as the average number of performances attended in the last year.

These different measures are related because changes in the overall level of consumption can be expressed as the product of the number of participants and the average frequency of participation. Moreover, changes in the number of participants, when expressed as a participation rate, may be due either to a change in behavior (a higher participation rate) or to a change in the size or composition of the population.

In fact, changes in total consumption levels may be due to any one of four different factors: changes in the size of the population, changes in the composition of the population, changes in the rate of participation among specific subgroups of the population, and changes in the frequency of participation for a subgroup. Understanding these distinctions is important because the conclusions one draws about how and why consumption patterns may be changing will differ depending upon the mechanism that is driving the change.

Changes due to growth in the size or composition of the population do not represent behavioral change but are by-products of broader population shifts. But changes due to participation rates indicate that the fraction of the population participating in the arts has itself changed. Changes due to increasing frequency of participation suggest not that more people have become involved in the arts but that current participants have changed their behavior. Because all these factors are likely to come into play, it is useful to understand these distinctions when attempting to understand changes in participation patterns.

Characteristics of Participants

In addition to understanding how levels of demand vary across forms of participation and discipline, it is also important to identify the sociodemographic and other characteristics associated with participation. Historically, education has proven to be the single best predictor of participation in the high arts, but studies have demonstrated that a variety of other attributes are also correlated with arts involvement (McCarthy et al., 2001).

Factors That Influence Participation

Finally, a number of factors influence patterns of demand in the aggregate. Although most empirical studies focus on who participates rather than why they participate, the following factors have been used to explain changes in participation patterns:

- sociodemographic changes, e.g., changes in the size and composition of the population

- changes in tastes, e.g., preferences for the arts and art forms

- changes in such practical considerations as the supply of artistic events and products, their cost, the availability of leisure time, income levels, and dissemination of information about the arts

- changes in the stock of individual experience with the arts (arts education, prior experience, knowledge).

SOURCES OF DATA

Two principal types of empirical data can be used to describe patterns of demand in the performing arts: survey data collected from representative samples of the population and aggregate attendance data on arts consumption based on administrative records. Survey data are collected in individual interviews and typically include information on the extent and types of individual involvement as well as on the social and economic characteristics of the individuals who are surveyed. The two major sources of these data are the Survey of Public Participation in the Arts (SPPA) sponsored by the National Endowment for the Arts (NEA, 1998a) and the Harris poll surveys conducted for Americans for the Arts

(Americans for the Arts, 1996). Each of these surveys has been conducted at more or less regular intervals and can be used to describe how participation patterns have been changing over time.

However, there are problems in estimating levels of participation using these data. Differences in questionnaire wording between the SPPA and Harris data, for example, limit the comparability of estimates between these two sources (Tepper, 1998, Robinson, 1989).[2] Moreover, because neither survey identifies the sector in which individuals participate, it is impossible to estimate directly how participation rates vary among the commercial, nonprofit, and volunteer sectors. Finally, changes in survey methods and a much higher refusal rate in the most recent SPPA make it difficult to compare the estimates based on the most recent data with those from earlier surveys (NEA, 1998a).

Administrative data collected by the national arts service organizations (NSOs) provide another source of data on consumption patterns. These data, typically collected on an annual basis, contain aggregate attendance figures for specific art forms and can be used to monitor how attendance patterns for specific disciplines change over time. Moreover, because membership in specific service agencies tends to be sector specific,[3] these data can be used to estimate attendance separately for the commercial and nonprofit sectors—although generally not for the volunteer sector.

However, there are several difficulties with these administrative data. First, they are not generally publicly available. Second, the classifications used to present them often change, making it difficult to analyze trends over time and across disciplines. Finally, because the data are provided on a voluntary basis by individual arts organizations, the number of organizations reporting often changes. Thus, it is impossible to distinguish whether changes in the aggregate attendance data are a result of changes in the number of organizations reporting or changes in total attendance patterns.

CURRENT PATTERNS OF DEMAND

Levels of Participation

As the historical review suggested, the performing arts are a popular leisure-time activity in America. According to the most recent survey of arts participation, about 42 percent of all Americans attended a performance in one of the

---

[2]The Harris polls, for example, ask whether individuals have ever participated in the arts, whereas the SPPA asks about participation in the last year. In addition, the Harris data make no distinction between levels of participation, whereas the SPPA data do.

[3]That is, commercial and nonprofit organizations generally belong to different service agencies.

seven performing arts in the preceding year (see Table 4.1).[4] This figure is slightly more than the proportion of the population who visited an art museum but considerably lower than those who read literature during this period. It is also well below the participation rate in more popular entertainment forms such as watching television, which is virtually universal, or attending films. Involvement in the performing arts also compares favorably with other leisure-time activities such as attending sporting events and camping, but is less popular than gardening and exercising.

At least in part, this comparison suggests that the popularity of these various activities is directly related to the degree to which they take place at a fixed time and place. Thus, television viewing—which is ideally suited to filling small bits of time, can be done simultaneously with other activities, and is available 24 hours a day—is not only universal but, in fact, consumes about three hours of every American's day (Robinson and Godbey, 1997). Similarly, activities like reading, exercising, and gardening, which individuals can fit into their schedules more or less when they choose, are more popular than those activities, such as attending a performing arts event, which are generally available only at a specific time and place.

How do these patterns of arts participation vary across the different sectors in which the arts are presented? Unfortunately, the SPPA data do not distinguish among consumption in the commercial, nonprofit, and volunteer sectors.

Table 4.1

Annual Participation Rates for Various Leisure-Time Activities

Activity	Participation Rate (percent)	Frequency/year
Arts-related		
Attended live performance	42.2	5.4
Visited art museum	34.9	3.3
Read literature	63.1	N/A
Popular entertainment		
Watched any TV	96.0	3 hr/day
Went to movie	65.5	9
Other leisure		
Went to sporting event	41.2	7
Exercised	75.7	N/A
Gardened	65.4	N/A
Camped, hiked, canoed	44.3	N/A

SOURCE: 1997 SPPA.

N/A = Not applicable.

---

[4]The seven performing arts are jazz, classical music, opera, musicals, non-musical plays, ballet, and other dance (NEA, 1998a).

However, as we will demonstrate in Chapter Six, with the exception of theater, the live performing arts are principally distributed in the nonprofit sector, whereas the reproduced arts are principally distributed through the commercial sector. Moreover, hands-on involvement in the arts at an amateur level principally takes place in the volunteer sector. Thus, sorting the reported levels of participation in the SPPA by form of involvement may be suggestive as to the levels of public participation by sector.

In this context, it is interesting to note that the 42 percent attendance rate in Table 4.1 compares with a participation rate of 78 percent of the population who listened or watched one of the seven performing arts in recorded form and the 67 percent personal or hands-on participation rate.[5] Moreover, the very high participation rates for television viewing and going to movies reflect the fact that the commercial performing-arts market is substantially larger than the nonprofit high-arts market.

Patterns of consumption of the performing arts vary not only by form of participation but also by discipline. Indeed, as Figure 4.1 indicates, participation rates (in whatever form) are lowest for opera and ballet, intermediate for classical music and jazz, and highest for theater and musicals. It is also interesting to note here that although participation rates for the performing arts as a whole exceed those for the visual arts, the participation rates for the visual arts for all types of involvement are higher than those for any single one of the performing arts.

Who Participates?

Education is by far the most powerful predictor of participation in the performing arts. Individuals with higher levels of education—especially college and graduate degrees—have much higher participation rates than others. This is true for each of the different forms of participation (see Figure 4.2).[6] The influence of education on participation, however, is not equal across all forms of participation. It is most pronounced among those who participate by attending the performing arts, somewhat less evident among those who participate through the media, and least pronounced among those who "do" art.

It is not entirely clear what drives this education effect. More highly educated individuals are more likely than others to have been exposed to the arts by

---

[5]The rate of personal participation is not limited to the performing arts but also includes such activities as writing, painting, sewing, etc. Thus, it is not directly comparable with the attendance and media rates. All three of these rates are based on 1997 SPPA data (NEA, 1998a).

[6]The effects of education on participation can also be observed across all disciplines (NEA, 1998a; Deveaux, 1994; Holak et al., 1986; Keegan, 1987; Lemmons, 1966).

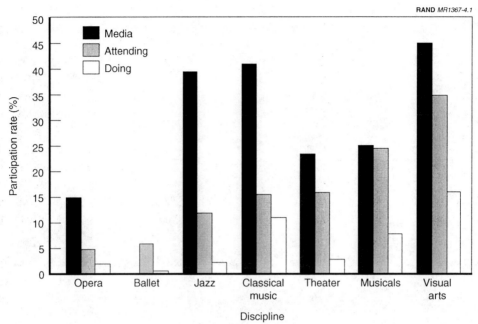

RAND *MR1367-4.1*

SOURCE: NEA, Survey of Public Participation in the Arts, 1997.

Figure 4.1—Rates of Participation in the Arts, by Discipline

family members during their childhood and to have taken courses in the arts during their schooling. This early exposure to the arts is important because familiarity and knowledge of the arts are directly related to participation rates (Orend and Keegan, 1996), as they are to most other types of leisure activity (Kelly and Freysinger, 2000). Indeed, Orend and Keegan find that arts appreciation classes taken during college have an even stronger effect on subsequent participation than those taken earlier. Education also helps individuals develop skill in dealing with the abstract—a skill that is useful for appreciating the arts (Toffler, 1964).[7]

However, because education seems to be more closely correlated with attendance than other forms of participation and attendance is the most social form of arts participation, more highly educated people may be more interested in the social dimensions of participation than are others. This correlation may

---

[7]Another possible explanation for this education effect is that it is really a by-product of the higher incomes associated with higher education levels because participation rates also tend to increase with income. However, studies indicate that after controlling for education, the association between participation and income is substantially reduced, indicating that education rather than income is the more important factor (Robinson et al., 1985; Robinson, 1993).

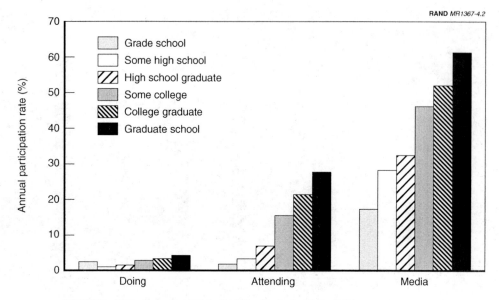

SOURCE: NEA, Survey of Public Participation in the Arts, 1997.

Figure 4.2—Education as a Correlate of Attendance

reflect a greater concern with the prestige attached to the arts or the documented tendency of the better educated to join a variety of associations of like-minded individuals—in this case, arts appreciators (Putnam, 2000).

The findings for other socioeconomic factors are more ambiguous. While gender (more women than men participate) and age also matter, they are less important than education. The effects of age, unlike education, appear to be most pronounced for hands-on participation, which is much more prevalent at younger ages (Peters and Cherbo, 1996). But rates of attendance and participation through the media do not vary significantly with age, after controlling for other factors—except for those over age 65. Other factors (e.g., marital status, political ideology, religion, income, and race) are generally not important after controlling for education.

In addition to sociodemographic variables, the literature also examines the relationship between participation and other background factors such as arts education and exposure to the arts as a child (Bergonzi and Smith, 1996; Orend and Keegan, 1996). These factors have been shown to be strongly associated with increases in attendance at live performances and in listening or watching recorded performances, and in the frequency with which individuals are involved in both of these activities. Moreover, these effects appear to hold even after controlling for levels of education. Indeed, Orend and Keegan suggest that the effects of arts socialization (in the form of both arts education classes and more general exposure to the arts) are particularly important in explaining differences in participation rates among the less well educated.

Finally, studies of the frequency with which the population participates in the performing arts suggest that the distribution of participation is highly skewed: A relatively small percentage of total attendees account for the vast majority of all visits. Indeed, those involved with the arts can generally be sorted into three categories: those who rarely, if ever, attend; those who infrequently attend; and those who are frequent attenders.[8]

The literature offers two slightly different explanations for this phenomenon. The economics literature, for example, suggests that the more knowledgeable people are about the arts, the more likely they are to participate, because they gain more satisfaction from a given level of consumption than do people who are less knowledgeable (Stigler and Becker, 1977). The leisure literature, on the other hand, tends to view this phenomenon more in psychological terms: A small fraction of the participants in leisure activities become serious "amateurs" for whom the activity becomes an end in itself (Stebbins, 1992). As Kelly and Freysinger (2000) point out, this phenomenon is common to a wide range of leisure activities in which there is a progression in commitment to the activity. In either case, this phenomenon helps to explain why the term "addiction" is sometimes used to describe the attraction of art lovers to the arts.

Why Do They Participate?

To understand the motivations for participation, three questions must be addressed. Why do people participate in the arts (rather than other leisure activities)? Why do they choose to become involved in different ways (doing, attending, or through the media)? And why do they choose specific art forms or disciplines? Each of these questions addresses a different aspect of demand. The first relates to the overall level of demand and the others refer to the ways that demand is distributed by form of participation (and thus sector) and discipline. Although a substantial literature addresses the first question, the latter two questions are rarely addressed.

By and large, studies of participants' motivations focus on the reasons individuals give for their decisions to attend or not attend performances (Ford, 1974; NEA, 1998a; Robinson, 1993). These studies highlight a variety of practical and

---

[8]The most comprehensive analysis of this phenomenon was conducted by Schuster (1991) for museum attendance. However, it has also been noted by Robinson et al. (1985) and Robinson (1993) for the performing arts. Orend and Keegan (1996) report a similar distinction in their comparisons of both attendance and participation through the media.

contextual factors—e.g., costs, availability, information, scheduling—that drive individual decisions but do not really explain why, in the aggregate, levels of demand change. Studies seeking to explain shifts in the overall level of demand, on the other hand, focus on factors that drive demand at the aggregate level. Four sets of factors, in particular, have been used to explain changes in overall demand: changes in the size and composition of the population; changes in peoples' taste for the arts; changes in practical factors such as availability, income, prices, and time that affect individuals' ability to pursue their preferences for the arts; and changes in the stock of knowledge about the arts. Such factors have been shown to affect participation in expected ways. For example, arts participation should increase as the population grows, as education levels increase, as the arts become more available or less expensive relative to alternative leisure pursuits, and as more people have exposure to the arts as children or in school.

Understanding the dynamic behind changes in tastes is less straightforward because it relates to a question that is not typically addressed in the literature: What are the underlying determinants of individual tastes? Individuals' preferences for the arts are typically assumed to be a function of their characteristics, such as education and income. Thus, changes in tastes are typically attributed to shifts in the composition of the population.

Even if we could predict the aggregate level of demand for the performing arts, however, we would not necessarily know how that demand will be distributed across sectors or particular art forms. To answer these questions we need to know why individuals choose to participate in the arts in different ways—an issue that has not been given much attention in the literature.

In considering the ways in which individuals choose to participate (and thus demand by market sector), Kelly and Freysinger (2000) have suggested that it may be useful to consider two different dimensions of individuals' choices: Are participants seeking entertainment or fulfillment? Do they prefer to participate alone or with others? Although this framework has not been subject to empirical testing, it suggests that combining these two dimensions can provide a framework for distinguishing among different types of art consumers (see Figure 4.3). Among those who are primarily seeking entertainment, individuals who are self-focused will be inclined to participate through the media, while those who are looking for a social experience will be casual attendees. For those primarily seeking enrichment, the self-focused participants will be inclined to hands-on participation, while those preferring to participate in groups will be "aficionado attendees."

Consumers falling into a particular cell of this classification scheme are not precluded from participating in the arts in other ways, since consumers whose

RAND *MR1367-4.3*

How	Why	
	Entertainment	Fulfillment
Self-focused	Media	Doing
Social	Attend (casual)	Attend (aficionado)

Figure 4.3—Explaining Participation Preferences

primary mode of participation is through the media may also attend live performances, as will those who "do" art. Moreover, regardless of how they choose to participate, individuals may choose from a wide variety of art forms, including both the high and the popular arts. This schema not only recognizes that the motivations for participating in the arts differ but, by recognizing that these motivations will influence the form that participation takes, provides a useful device for segmenting that demand. Participation through the media or recorded arts, for example, not only is the most popular form of participation, it is also most likely to occur in the commercial sector where the recorded arts are most likely to be distributed. Participation by doing, on the other hand, is more likely to occur in the volunteer sector.

The market for the live performing arts, which are typically produced in the nonprofit sector, consists of two distinct groups of consumers: those who are casual attendees and those who are aficionados, or enthusiastic fans of the arts. The former differ from the latter not only in their motivations but also in their numbers, their knowledge of the arts, and, in all probability, their tastes. The aficionados are the frequent attendees discussed above: a small and select group who are likely to be knowledgeable and interested in a diverse array of content and the aesthetics of the art experience. In contrast, the casual attendees are likely to be far more numerous, less interested in the art form per se, and more likely to be attracted to more traditional fare. By identifying how motivations affect the structure of demand, this schema provides a basis for suggesting why these patterns may change in the future.

Very little is known about why arts participants choose one art form over another. The literature on individual motivations indicates that interest in the material programmed is a relatively important factor in the decision to attend specific performances (Ford Foundation, 1974), but this fact does not explain why individuals prefer one art form to another. An individual's ability to tailor his or her participation according to his or her own schedule and tastes, as we suggested above, may also play a role. The fact that attendance at art museums is greater than attendance at any of the performing arts may in part be due to this phenomenon. How relevant the programmed material is to the participant is also likely to play a role, but this connection has not been researched.

KEY TRENDS

More Attendees but Stable Rates of Attendance

Despite the fact that total attendance at live performances has been increasing, rates of attendance (the percentage of the population attending performances) have mostly been stable. The most recent SPPA data indicate, for example, that total attendance at live performances increased 4–16 percent between 1982 and 1997 (see Figure 4.4).[9] This increase is evident among all the live performing arts—although the extent of the increase differs. The vast majority of the increase occurred between 1992 and 1997. However, changes in survey

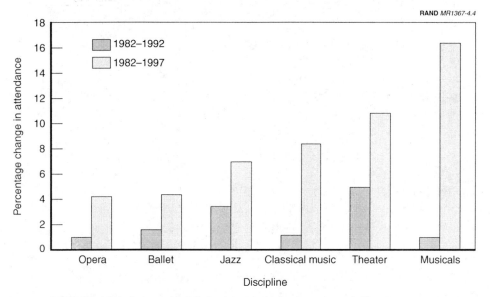

SOURCE: NEA, Survey of Public Participation in the Arts, 1982, 1992, 1997.

Figure 4.4—Gains in Attendance by Discipline, 1982–1997

---

[9]The estimates reported in this section are based on SPPA surveys. Participation is defined as "(1) attending a performance or visiting an art museum or gallery (attendance); (2) listening or watching an arts performance or program on radio, television, video cassette or disk, phonograph record, tape recording, compact disk, or personal computer (participation via media); (3) performing art for oneself or in public or creating a work of art for oneself or for exhibition to the public (personal participation)." The attendance figures exclude elementary, middle, or high school performances. Respondents supply their own definitions of art and artistic disciplines (NEA, 1998a, p. 12).

procedures and a much higher refusal rate in the 1997 survey cast the size of this increase into doubt—it is not clear how much of this increase is a result of changed survey procedures and how much represents true behavioral change (NEA, 1998a).[10]

Moreover, as we noted in the introduction to this chapter, increases in total attendance levels may be due to any one of four factors: changes in the size and composition of the population, changes in rate of participation, and changes in the frequency of attendance among participants. Unfortunately, the frequency data from the 1997 SPPA survey are not directly comparable with earlier data, so we cannot determine how much of the change in total attendance results from changes in the frequency with which participants attended the live performing arts.

We can, however, identify the effects of population growth and increasing education levels on total attendance.[11] As Figure 4.5 indicates, most of the increase in attendance between 1982 and 1997 was the result of population growth and increasing education levels—not an increase in the rate at which people participate in the arts. Indeed, between 1982 and 1992, attendance ratios actually went down for all six of the disciplines examined.[12] Thus, although total attendance has been rising, the rate of attendance at live performances has mostly been stable. If these trends continue, slower population growth and shifts in the composition of the population (both of which can be expected) could eventually produce a drop in total attendance.

Increases in the supply and geographic availability of the live performing arts have also played a role in the absolute increase in attendance levels. As noted in the prior section, the resurgence in the live performing arts initially triggered by the Ford Foundation's investment in the arts produced a dramatic increase in the number and geographic dispersion of live arts performances.[13]

---

[10]Of these two factors, the increase in the refusal rate is probably the most important. The earlier SPPA surveys were administered as a supplement to a Crime Victimization Survey and this appears to have elicited the cooperation of a broader cross-section of respondents, whereas the 1997 survey was administered as a separate instrument and, as a result, appears to have resulted in a higher response rate by individuals who were arts participants.

[11]In other words, changes in total attendance levels can be disaggregated into changes in the size of the total population, changes in the proportion of the population in particular educational categories, and changes in the attendance rates within each of these educational categories.

[12]That is, the changes in total arts attendance between 1982 and 1992 were due exclusively to population growth and increasing education levels; the rates at which different education groups attended declined during this period.

[13]The increase in the geographic distribution of the live performing arts is documented in NEA (1998a). The increase in the number of performances is discussed in general terms in Kreidler (1996). In addition, data reported by the various arts service organizations indicate that between 1985 and 1995, the number of symphonic performances, for example, increased by 50 percent.

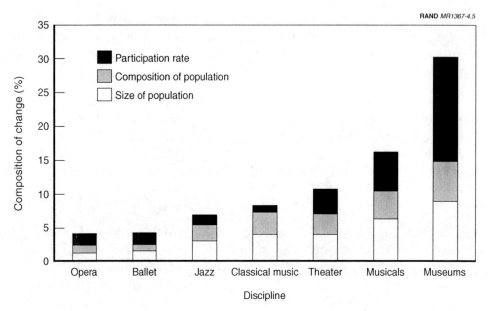

SOURCE: NEA, Survey of Public Participation in the Arts, 1982 and 1997.

Figure 4.5—Composition of Change in Attendance by Discipline, 1982–1997

Why this increase in availability was not matched by a corresponding increase in attendance rates is not altogether clear. Among the potential contributing factors are increasing competition from other leisure activities, increasing ticket prices, and changing leisure patterns, as we discuss later in this section.

Another possible factor, which has not been adequately researched, is arts education. As we have already noted, arts education seems to play a crucial role in creating audiences for the arts. However, we have very little good information on patterns of arts education and how they may have been changing. Arts education, for example, may take several different forms depending upon the purpose and level of the instruction. Although a good deal of artistic instruction takes place in private lessons outside school, many elementary and secondary schools provide music, dancing, and acting lessons as a way of introducing students to the arts. Some of those who take these lessons later pursue additional training at higher levels on a vocational or avocational basis. In addition, many schools and institutions of higher learning offer arts appreciation courses, and some educational institutions train arts teachers. Although the SPPA (and other participation surveys) provides information on individuals' arts education experiences, very little systematic research appears to have been done on the suppliers of arts education beyond studies of arts education in the primary and secondary schools. The evidence that does exist suggests that although the frequency of arts education in the schools may have increased slightly between 1962 and 1989, the amount of class time devoted to it has actually declined (Leonhard, 1991). It is also clear that school-based arts education programs are much more prevalent for music and the visual arts than they are for theater or dance—a factor that may contribute to the differential popularity of these art forms. We also know that arts education programs are much more prevalent in large schools than small schools. Unfortunately, we have no comprehensive data on what has been happening to such programs since 1990.

Growing Participation Through the Media

In contrast to the stability of attendance rates, participation through the media has been increasing dramatically in practically every discipline. Figure 4.6 shows the percentage point difference in media and live attendance rates in 1982, 1992, and 1997. To take the example of classical music, the figure shows that in 1982 participation through the media was 7 percentage points higher than attendance rates; by 1997 that gap was over 25 percent—an increase of nearly 20 percentage points. In all cases, media consumption has increased in the 1992–1997 period. Although the trend from 1982 to 1992 is more ambiguous, it still tends to favor media participation.

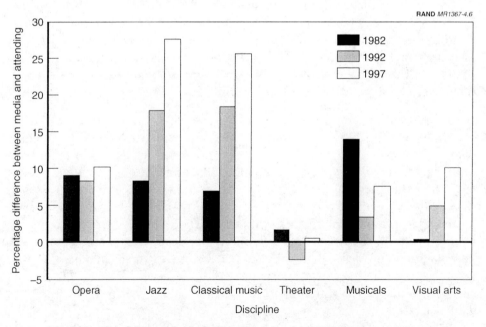

SOURCE: NEA, Survey of Public Participation in the Arts, 1982, 1992, and 1997.

Figure 4.6—Growth of Participation in the Arts Through the Media, 1982–1997

Besides the obvious explanation that the quality of electronically reproduced substitutes for the performing arts has increased dramatically, we can also explain this trend as a function of the rising relative price of attending a live performance. Two factors drive this price. The first is the direct cost of attending, e.g., ticket prices, transportation, and childcare. From 1980 to 1995, the real price of entertainment services rose 28 percent more than did the Consumer Price Index. The second is the opportunity cost of attending the live performing arts, which is a time-intensive activity.

The opportunity costs of attending live performances might be greater than watching or listening to the same program through the media for three reasons. First, attending a live event typically includes preparation and travel time that a recorded performance does not. Second, individuals can often choose to experience a recorded performance in more than one sitting. Finally, and probably more important, unlike a live performance which takes place at a specific time and place, individuals can often choose when and where they want to experience a recorded performance.

Of course, a central question about the growing popularity of participation through the media is the degree to which individuals view recorded and live performances as substitutes. Certainly, many arts enthusiasts maintain that they are not comparable experiences despite improvements in recording technology. Moreover, as we suggested above, watching or listening to a recorded performance at home lacks the social dimension that motivates many individuals to attend live performances. Unfortunately, without a better understanding of why individuals choose to participate in the arts in one form rather than another, we cannot really answer that question.

We do know, however, that there is much less crossover among forms of participation than we might expect. Crossover effects in arts participation could come about in one of two ways: (1) a person who takes part in the arts through one form of participation may be more inclined to take part through another form—e.g., if he participates through the media (say, watches a program on television), he may be more apt to attend a live arts performance; and (2) a person who participates in a particular type of art may be more inclined to participate in another—e.g., if she attends live symphony performances, she may be more likely to attend musicals. In a major study of crossover effects in the arts, Love (1995) argues that crossover effects are more the exception than the rule—suggesting that these different forms of participation appeal to different audiences.[14]

---

[14]It should be noted, however, that the structure of these comparisons may have influenced this result. Love compared the percentage of people who participated in the more frequent activity (participation through the media) with those who also attended live performances and found a low

Consumer Desire for Greater Flexibility

The two prior trends are symptomatic of a third: Americans appear to be placing an increasing premium on flexibility in their consumption of the arts. That is, they will tend to favor art forms and modes of participation that allow them to determine what they consume, when they consume it, and how they consume it—sometimes referred to as "consumption by appointment." Thus, media consumption may well dominate attendance because it is more amenable to the individual's schedule. Similarly, art forms that allow individuals to decide exactly what and how much they consume will be more popular than those that do not. This point is consistent with trends in live attendance from 1982 to 1997 in different disciplines. The rate of growth of art museum attendance, for example, has outstripped that of all the performing arts throughout this period.

A major reason for this pattern may well be the changing availability of leisure time in American society. Although the growth in leisure time that Americans enjoyed for much of the 20th century has reversed for some segments of the population, it is unclear whether this is true for Americans in general. Robinson and Godbey (1997), for example, argue that with a few notable exceptions, Americans have at least as much leisure time as in the past. Schor (1991) argues the reverse. Most observers agree, however, that as a result of irregular working schedules the structure of free time has become increasingly fragmented—especially for the more highly educated who are the heaviest consumers of the arts. The perception of reduced leisure time and the increasingly home-centered focus of leisure activities have no doubt increased the competition that live performances face from other leisure-time pursuits (Putnam, 2000).

FUTURE ISSUES

The key question for the future is how demand will change, both in the aggregate and in terms of the different market segments we identified above.

Demographic Changes

Improvements in education levels that have marked the past 30 years can be expected to continue, although in all likelihood at a slower rate. This trend bodes well for the performing arts. The aging of the population associated with the maturation of the baby boomers may also play a role in influencing future

---

correlation. The results might have been somewhat different had he focused on the percentage of people in the less frequent activity (attending live performances) who also participated through the media.

patterns of demand, but its effects are less clear. Age can affect participation patterns in two ways. First, participation patterns change as people get older. Age matters most for direct or hands-on participation, in which younger adults are substantially more likely to participate than others (Peters and Cherbo, 1996). Its effects on participation through the media and attendance at live performances are not particularly pronounced until after 65, when all forms of participation drop markedly.

Second, behavior changes not only as people age but as they are replaced in the population by younger cohorts. Some studies suggest that the rate of arts participation among the later cohorts of the baby boom is substantially lower than that of their parents (Peterson et al., 1999). If this pattern persists as these cohorts approach middle age, it may not bode well for future participation in the performing arts. A second cohort effect relates to the ways in which the population will participate in the arts. Today's youth, for example, are much more comfortable with computers, VCRs, and other technologies than are their parents. When they reach the prime arts-consumption years, they will be more likely than their predecessors to rely on the media and Web-based entertainment.

A third demographic change that we can expect will occur in the ethnic composition of the population. Currently, close to 40 percent of America's total population growth is attributable to immigration (McCarthy and Vernez, 1996). If this trend continues, as we anticipate, it will increase the ethnic diversification of the population. And although ethnicity is only one factor influencing artistic tastes, increasing ethnic diversification could spur demand for a greater variety of art forms and styles by expanding existing markets and exposing the wider population to a greater variety of artistic styles, just as it has diversified American cuisine.

Economic Changes

In addition to these demographic changes, rising income levels and changing leisure patterns can also be expected to affect the demand for the performing arts. Dramatic increases in women's labor force participation and education levels, combined with recent improvements in productivity, have produced a sustained rise in Americans' disposable incomes. Ordinarily, one would expect higher incomes to spur demand for art since rising incomes enable participants to spend more on the arts. The net effects of rising incomes may, however, be partly offset by the fact that as wage rates increase, people's time becomes more valuable and they tend to become more sensitive to how their leisure activities fit with their schedules and their available free time. This effect, referred to as the opportunity costs of rising incomes, may well have less influence on overall demand than on how individuals choose to participate in the arts. The rising opportunity cost of time is likely to intensify the preference for flexible activities that can be tailored to individual schedules and tastes. This phenomenon would appear to favor consumption through the media rather than attendance. Indeed, if Americans' leisure time continues to shrink and become more fragmented, this trend will intensify.

The Role of Technology

Technology will also play a role in shaping future demand for the arts. Continued advances in e-commerce and digital technology seem likely to affect future demand in two ways. First, they will allow individuals to increasingly personalize their consumption so that they can experience the kinds of art they want, when they want, and where they want. This may well mean a more individualized and self-focused approach to arts consumption, and therefore an increase in demand for niche markets. Indeed, the Internet and various forms of e-commerce will facilitate consumption tailored to individual tastes by promoting direct interchange both between artists and consumers (thus reducing dependence upon traditional retailers and live performing arts venues) and among consumers who share an interest in specialized forms of art. The net effect of these developments will be that the market for new products and types of art will be increasingly freed from the geographic constraints imposed by the need for market thresholds sufficient to support production and distribution.

In addition, continued technological advances seem certain to promote increases in arts participation both through the media and by direct involvement in creating art. The former effect will be spurred by improvements in reproduction and transmission technologies that reduce the aesthetic disadvantages of non-live performances. The latter effect could be driven by new technologies that provide new ways, such as new media art forms, for individuals to create art themselves.

How these changes will affect the demand for the live performing arts is not altogether clear and may well depend upon the degree to which aesthetic versus social factors drive future demand, and the extent to which the public views recorded and live performances as substitutes. To the extent that audiences for live performances are dominated by casual attendees who are seeking social interaction with others interested in the arts, demand for the live performing arts may hold up well. However, if the above factors drive demand, the market for new and innovative work could well decline.

In sum, the future could promise an increase in demand for the performing arts. But that increase will not necessarily be felt evenly across forms of participation, sectors, or disciplines. A combination of social, economic, and technological changes could well bring more benefit to consumption through the media and direct involvement in the creative process. Moreover, these changes seem likely to facilitate the development of a variety of niche and specialized markets as individuals have the incentive and the means to tailor their consumption to their individual tastes, regardless of where they live or what is available in their local markets.

Chapter Five

ARTISTS: CREATORS AND PERFORMERS

In the performing arts, artists are either creators of works of art—such as composers, playwrights, and choreographers—or performers—such as musicians, conductors, actors, and directors. Sometimes they are both. Although they are at the core of the performing arts, artists are difficult to classify. For example, we don't know exactly how to distinguish professional artists from those who pursue the performing arts on a part-time or avocational basis. Nor do we know what roles these different types of artists play in the production of the performing arts in its various sectors and with what consequences for the quality and amount of performing arts available to the public. Although we have good reasons to believe that a career in the performing arts differs from a career in other occupations (Alper and Wassall, 2000), we don't really know how careers for artists in the commercial and nonprofit sectors differ or how much artists move among sectors. Some artistic talents may be more interchangeable between "high" and "popular" arts activity than others.

Over the last century, the artistic profession has been growing in both reputation and population. Although performance was a respectable avocation for the leisure class before the 19th century, professional performing artists were often held in low esteem. With the emergence of the popular film industry in the early 20th century, however, actors and actresses experienced soaring popularity and incomes. While the cachet of the leisure-class amateur eroded, the stature of professional performing artists began to rise, both in the commercial popular arts and the nonprofit high arts. The Ford era brought heavy investments in new conservatories and other training programs from the 1960s to the 1980s, which allowed artists of all kinds to develop their talents more fully and to specialize in specific disciplines and performance areas.

Increased professionalism, combined with changing marketing practices in the arts, has also promoted the emergence of superstar artists who have come to rival their counterparts in sports in terms of the salaries and prestige they garner. Although stardom is hardly a new phenomenon in the arts (Levine, 1988), the reach and rewards of stardom seem to be increasing (Frank and Cook, 1995).

As we will show, the number of people who call themselves professional artists has been growing for decades, despite the difficulties they often face in sustaining full-time employment in the arts. Although we have no systematic data on levels of amateur participation in the arts for most of the 20th century, Toffler (1964) asserts the number of amateurs increased sharply during the 1950s, and more recent participation data suggest that more people are taking up music, theater, and dance in their free time. Such trends are important to any discussion of artists because amateurs outnumber professionals by a factor of 20 or 30 to 1,[1] and thus play an important role in the delivery of the performing arts.

This chapter describes what we know about performing artists as a group and by discipline, first by clarifying the distinctions between professionals and amateurs and describing the data available on artists, then by describing the characteristics of artists and artistic employment and how they compare with other professionals and careers. At the end of the chapter, we identify changes in the environment that are likely to affect performing artists in the future.

KEY CONCEPTS

As we suggested above, the initial challenge in analyzing performing artists is to define who they are. In the data, they are characterized as belonging to two categories: professionals and amateurs. But this simple dichotomy fails to capture the range of careers in the arts that fall between full-time professionals and hobbyists. Most artistic careers are composites, consisting of paid arts work, unpaid arts work, and non-arts work (Throsby, 1996, Ruttenberg et al., 1978; Alper et al., 1996). As a result, the artistic labor force is notably fluid, with a large number of part-time employees who move between arts-related and non-arts-related employment. Therefore, defining professionals as those artists with full-time employment in the arts would be too restrictive.

Moreover, it is not always easy to delineate the difference between professional and amateur activity. Some commentators use the term "professional" to indicate high standards of competence. Apart from the obvious difficulty of measuring skill levels in the arts, this approach is less useful in a labor market where there are so many highly trained artists working in multiple environments—including commercial, nonprofit, and volunteer settings—and where there are so many professional performances of mixed quality.

Because we are constrained by the way the data on artists are reported, we use the term professional in this analysis to mean artists who pursue art as their vo-

---

[1]Estimates of amateur participation based on the General Social Survey put the ratio as 30:1. Those based on the SPPA suggest it may be closer to 20:1.

cation and amateurs as those who practice their art on an avocational basis. However, a more appropriate taxonomy of artistic careers would include a fuller range of categories, including casual hobbyists, amateur aficionados, part-time professionals, full-time professionals, and superstars. The distinctions among these categories would be based on multiple criteria, including artists' educational qualifications, membership in credentialing bodies, income earned, amount of time devoted to performing, and peer acceptance.[2]

DATA SOURCES

Three types of data are needed to answer the questions we have posed in this chapter: information on (1) the characteristics of artists, (2) the institutions that employ them, and (3) the dynamics of their careers. Almost all the data available on artists, however, fall into the first category. Data on career dynamics and the experience of artists over time do not currently exist, and very little information is available on the employment decisions or conditions of artists in different institutional settings.

Data collected on artists focus mostly on self-defined professional artists, particularly their sociodemographic and employment characteristics, although amateur activity is also captured in some survey data. Most of the information on professional artists comes from one of three sources:

- the Decennial Census of Population, which includes a detailed battery of questions about individuals' employment and sociodemographic characteristics[3]

- the monthly Current Population Survey (CPS), jointly sponsored by the Bureau of the Census and the Bureau of Labor Statistics, which fields a standard battery of questions about employment to a much smaller national sample of the population

- regular studies commissioned by the NEA's Research Division, which supplement Population Census data by providing more detail on artists' employment and earnings.

In each of these sources, professionals are identified as those who call themselves professionals. There is no way to verify from the data whether those who claim to be professional artists actually earn income from their activity. Nor can

---

[2]We are indebted to David Throsby for his suggestions on the distinction among categories of artists.

[3]Data in this report come primarily from the 1990 Population Census. 2000 Population Census data on occupations are not yet available at this writing.

we tell what proportion of their income is derived from the arts. Therefore, we can only speculate about the career dynamics of the profession based largely on the collective accounts of individual artists.

The two major sources of information on amateurs are the General Social Survey and the NEA's Survey of Public Participation in the Arts. In both of these surveys, amateurs are identified by their responses to questions about their leisure activities. Amateur performing artists are those who have created or performed in an artistic production in their leisure time—whether in private or before a public audience.[4] Because the questions do not ask respondents to describe their degree of involvement in these activities, we cannot distinguish the casual hobbyist from the professional who also engages in the arts as a leisure activity.

CURRENT PICTURE

Artists' Characteristics

Performing Artists Represent a Small Proportion of All Artists

The 1990 Census of Population counted 1.6 million artists, who constituted 1.3 percent of the nation's workforce. They are categorized into four broad types, as shown in Figure 5.1. The majority of those the Census includes within the artist category are graphic designers and architects—occupations that are not generally involved in the creation of either popular or high arts. Performing artists constituted only 17 percent of all artists—considerably more than the number of authors but fewer than the population of visual artists. Musicians and composers make up more than half of all performing artists, followed by actors and directors (39 percent) and dancers (8 percent).

Performing Artists Resemble Other Professional Workers

Census data also indicate that performing artists are, on average, about six years older, more likely to have a college degree, and more likely to be white than is the average American worker. However, these differences generally disappear when they are compared with all professional and technical workers—a more appropriate comparison given the comparable levels of education among these two groups (Throsby, 1994). One difference that does persist, however, is gender—whereas only 52 percent of professional and technical workers are male, 60 percent of performing artists are men.

---

[4]The SPPA data suggest that the percentage of amateurs who perform in public varies substantially by discipline—from a high of 60 percent for ballet dancers to a low of 10 percent for those who play a classical instrument. No distinction is drawn between paid and free admissions (NEA, 1998a).

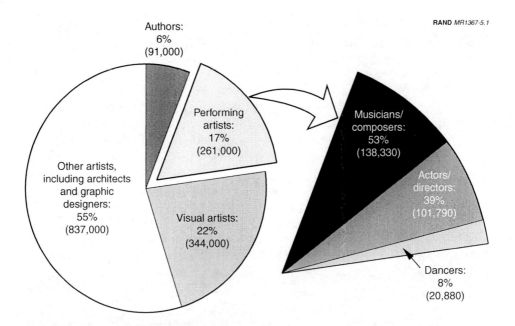

Figure 5.1—Proportion of All Artists Who Are Performing Artists

We can also make selective comparisons between amateurs and professionals in terms of their sociodemographic characteristics. In general, amateurs tend to be somewhat older, better educated, more likely to be female, and less likely to be white than are professionals. Although it is very difficult to compare the incomes of amateurs and professionals for the reasons cited above, the data show that amateurs, not surprisingly, have incomes comparable with that of the general population.[5]

Employment

Performing Artists Face More Difficult Employment Circumstances Than Do Most Other Professionals

As we noted above, analysis of artists' employment circumstances is complicated by the fact that artists are typically employed—at least part-time—in non-arts jobs. About three-quarters of all artists hold non-arts jobs at least part of the time (Alper et al., 1996).[6] Although we cannot determine how much of their

---

[5]These comparisons are based on computations from the U.S. Census and the General Social Survey.

[6]A 1977 survey of performing artists indicated that only one-third of those surveyed managed to work full-time in the arts (Ruttenberg et al., 1978).

income is arts-related, it is nevertheless interesting to examine the data for distinctions across disciplines and across professions (see Table 5.1).

Focusing first on performing artists, the data show that the average earnings of actors and directors ($22,000) was more than twice as high as the earnings of other performing artists. Actors and directors were employed more weeks out of the year than other performing artists but faced higher unemployment rates (13.2 percent). Musicians and composers earned substantially less ($10,000) and worked somewhat fewer weeks (48), but were less likely to be unemployed (4.0 percent). Dancers had the lowest annual earnings ($8,500), worked the fewest weeks (39), and experienced high unemployment rates (9.1 percent).[7]

When compared with authors, performing artists appear to be at a distinct disadvantage. Authors earned more than actors and directors—the highest-paid performing artists—while working about the same number of weeks and experiencing much lower unemployment. In comparison with workers in general, performing artists in the aggregate earn less, work fewer weeks, and face higher unemployment. The disadvantages performing artists experience in the labor force are even more pronounced when artists are compared with professional and technical workers, whose education levels are closer to theirs than they are to the labor force as a whole.

It should be noted here, however, that the employment profile of performing artists looks good compared with that of visual artists. A 1982 NEA report describing the lives of visual artists in four major cities found that the median annual income of artists from art sales, commissions, and grants or awards was $718, with only 8.5 percent earning over $10,000 (NEA, 1982a). Median production costs, on the other hand, were $1,450, about twice the median

Table 5.1

Employment Characteristics of Performing Artists Compared with Other Professions

Profession	Median Annual Wage (1989)	Median Weeks of Full-Time Work (2000)	Unemployment Rate (percent) (2000)
Musicians and composers	$10,000	48	4.0
Actors and directors	$22,000	50	13.2
Dancers	$8,500	39	9.1
Authors	$23,000	49	2.3
Professional and technical workers	$24,000	52	2.4
All workers	$22,000	52	6.7

SOURCES: Bureau of Labor Statistics, U.S. Census, Current Population Survey.

---

[7]These data are based on 1990 Population Census figures. The earnings figures are for 1989 (Alper and Wassall, 2000). See also Ellis and Beresford, 1994.

income. Over a quarter of visual artists reported earning nothing at all from their art over a three-year period during which they had exhibited (Kreidler, 1996).

Of course, the salary figures from the Census of Population data in Table 5.1 reflect both arts and non-arts income, so they are not directly comparable with the income figures cited in the NEA report. In fact, the incomes based on the Census may tell us as much about the different types of jobs artists hold outside the arts as about the differences in what they earn from their artistic careers. Authors, for example, who work primarily in professional and education services, earn more than performing artists, who are more likely to work in low-skilled service industries (Throsby and Thompson, 1994).

These types of comparisons are often cited as the basis for the image of the "starving artist" that abounds in some circles. Filer (1986) disputes this portrait, noting that when all sources of income and spousal support are included, the differences in income between artists and other workers largely disappear. If, however, non-arts employment represents a form of underemployment for performing artists because it is outside their chosen profession, then the un-employment comparisons reported above greatly underestimate the true extent of underemployment in the performing arts. It seems clear that artists need to rely on multiple sources and types of employment to make ends meet.

This employment picture is drawn, of course, from the *average* experience of performing artists; as such, it does not tell us about the experience of individual artists. As we discuss later in this chapter, the presence of the superstars is a strong force in the arts labor market. Although these stars represent a tiny fraction of the entire professional workforce, they offer a powerful incentive for aspiring young artists to stay in the profession.

Career Dynamics

Careers in the Performing Arts Differ from Other Careers

A career in the performing arts differs from most other careers, especially professional and technical occupations. It is perhaps more like a career in professional sports than it is like other professions. Although athletic and artistic activities are in most ways quite different, their career dynamics have a number of similarities. First, the earnings of artists tend to peak early and decline more quickly than in other professions (Brooks, 1994).[8] Second, artists' employment,

---

[8]This phenomenon will vary somewhat for different types of artists. It is more likely to be apparent for performers whose art is directly dependent upon their physical abilities, e.g., dancers. Its effects

like that of athletes, is sporadic and fragmented. Most artists work in day jobs only up to the point of securing subsistence. The data show that most performers work for multiple employers during the year. One study (Ruttenberg et al., 1978) has shown that only one in five performing artists worked for the same employer throughout the year and some worked for as many as ten employers. Third, most artists leave their profession early—typically in their mid-thirties— as career mobility decreases (Menger, 1999). Fourth, musicians and certain other performers are vulnerable to injuries from repeated practice and performance; these injuries sometimes cut promising careers short. Fifth, many performing arts jobs and casting agencies are concentrated geographically, placing constraints on artists seeking employment. For example, 70 percent of the members of Actors Equity reside in New York and California. Finally, like athletes, very few artists make it big in their field but many are inspired by the success of superstars.

Those who enter the arts appear to be motivated by powerful incentives—a love of the arts and the pleasure they derive from creation and performance. Artistic careers may well offer greater non-monetary rewards, such as lifestyle and fulfillment, than do other careers (Jeffri, 1998). Nevertheless, it is not surprising that many artists leave the profession at a relatively young age or decide to pursue their interest in the arts on a part-time or amateur basis. Particularly as income pressures increase with the demands of families and child-rearing, many young artists reassess their career choices and consider whether they would be better off in a more stable career. As we will discuss in the next chapter, because most performing arts organizations in the nonprofit and volunteer sectors are very small and rely on heavily discounted or volunteer labor for their existence, we predict a steady and growing demand for those performing artists who are willing to perform outside professional ranks.

Formal Arts Education Plays a Distinctive Role

Another distinctive feature of a career in the performing arts is the relative importance of education and experience in career advancement. In most professional careers, education plays a critical role in gaining access to jobs, and work experience determines the rate of advancement (Economic Report of the President, 1997). In the arts, despite the fact that formal education levels are comparable with those of other occupations, experience seems more important than education both for finding employment and advancing in one's career (Throsby, 1994).

---

in artists' earnings data will also be offset because less successful artists, and thus those with the lowest earnings, abandon their careers earliest.

This feature of artistic careers has created ambivalence within the arts policy community about the emphasis to place on training artists. From 1966 to 1981, the NEA made only token efforts toward educating artists. In 1982, however, then–NEA Chairman Frank Hodsoll made arts education a top agency priority. Hodsoll's initiative had two components: first, to promote arts appreciation, especially in schools; and second, to develop programs to train artists and arts educators (Myers and Brooks, forthcoming). The latter initiative is most relevant here. But given the importance of experience to advancement in artistic careers, it is not entirely clear how to achieve a balance between education and job training within a traditional educational environment. Moreover, arts educators have complained that the NEA's efforts rely too much on artists and too little on arts educators (Smith, 1992). In any case, charitable giving has tended to shy away from most arts education programs, preferring instead to support artists and performing groups. This led the Music Educators National Conference to complain that ". . . there has been no evidence that the corporate or foundation communities have particular interest in considering the traditional arts education community as a full partner in the national arts enterprise" (Music Educators National Conference, 1986, p. 10).

KEY TRENDS

Increasing Prominence of Superstars

As we have noted above, there is tremendous variation in the wages of artists, with the rare superstar earning millions of dollars a year and the average artist making little more than the minimum wage. This phenomenon is referred to as a "superstar market." Superstar markets exist in labor markets where small differences in ability lead to large differences in compensation. This occurs when information about talent becomes so accurate—or marketing of a particular artist as "the best" so common—that demand coalesces around a very few stars, driving their wages far above those of everyone else in the field (Frank and Cook, 1995; Rosen, 1982).

Although there is little empirical research on this phenomenon in the performing arts, the anecdotal wisdom on this point is unambiguous: the performing arts are experiencing a polarization in earnings in which a few artists earn huge rewards while most artists earn very little. We suspect that there are two reasons for this development. First, technological advances in reproduction and distribution have dramatically expanded the market for successful artists and have also made it possible to know the field and discern subtle differences in artistic ability. Second, and perhaps more important, marketing efforts to build star power have become ever more pervasive because the potential rewards of market success are so great.

More Artists, Fewer Job Opportunities

Since 1970, the supply of professional artists has increased dramatically. This point is documented in Figure 5.2, which depicts the increase in the number of self-proclaimed professional artists (and their rising share of the labor force) between 1970 and 1990. The total number of artists approximately doubled over this period. Corrected for growth in population, the increase was still over 40 percent. Although the available evidence suggests that unemployment among artists was lower than for the civilian workforce (5.3 percent versus 6.7 percent in 1991), and that the unemployment rate among artists fell by 0.7 percent from 1983 to 1991, these comparisons, as we noted above, include all labor force activity by artists and thus may underestimate the true extent of unemployment and underemployment in the performing arts. Indeed, the *number* of unemployed artists has increased over this period (Menger, 1999).

These data exclude the large number of individuals who are amateur composers, actors, performers, and dancers. What options exist for these individuals and for the increasing number of professional artists? As we will show, the number of nonprofit arts organizations has expanded dramatically over the

RAND *MR1367-5.2*

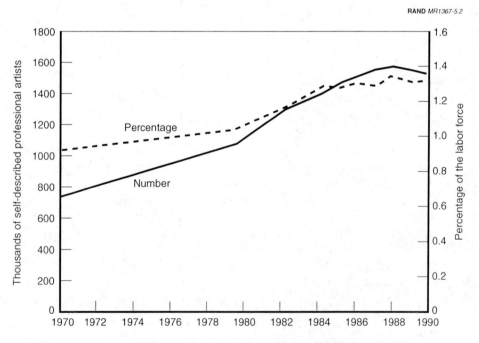

SOURCE: U.S. Census, Current Population Survey.

Figure 5.2—Growth in the Number of Professional Artists, 1970–1990

past two decades—primarily as a result of a burgeoning of small organizations. We suspect, although we cannot document empirically, that many of these performers are working as volunteers or for heavily discounted wages in these organizations, many of which are in the volunteer sector.

As we have suggested throughout this chapter, the ability of performing artists to practice their craft has generally been conditioned by the willingness of arts organizations and producers to employ them. This situation reflects the traditional structure of the performing arts in which producers and distributors intervene between artists and audiences by determining what arts will be produced and how.

This situation has been changing as recent technological advances dramatically increase artists' access to modes of production. Specifically, the advent of the Internet, web-based e-commerce, and the dramatic improvements in reproduction technology and broad-band transmission are making it easier for composers and musicians, for example, to produce their own recordings, identify and reach potential audiences, and thus promote and distribute their material without relying on established firms. These new technologies have lowered the entry barriers that producers traditionally imposed on composers and performers, who can now produce and distribute their work on their own (Larson, 1997; Seabrook, 2000).

Although these changes may be most feasible in the short run for specialized niche markets, they offer at least the prospect of later expansion to wider, more popular markets if they can first generate sufficient momentum in more specialized niche markets. For example, several Internet services such as InterneTV mix artist-submitted performing arts material with standards and classics, creating a venue that does not classify work according to preconceived levels of fame or fortune.[9]

However, the very ease of entry provided by the new technology, which enables motivated individuals to gain access to artistic material they formerly could not have found, may impose a new intermediary between artists and audiences. As more artists seek to avail themselves of this new technology, the very proliferation of new artists and their products may overload audiences who find that they require intermediaries to alert them to the voices they want to hear. Traditionally, record companies have served this function, focusing consumers' attention on those artists and material that they believe will have the broadest market. If a new set of marketers increasingly substitutes for the traditional intermediaries, it is not clear what criteria they will use to highlight specific artists and what the implications will be for the type and quality of art.

---

[9]See http://www.internetv.com/.

Intellectual Property Questions Created by New Technologies

Although new technologies such as the Internet are making it easier for some performing artists—particularly musicians—to promote and distribute as well as create and perform their own material, they are also reviving old questions about who should own the legal rights to creative intellectual property. According to Litman (1996),

> Our current copyright law is based on a model devised for print media, and expanded with some difficulty to embrace a world that includes live, filmed and taped performances, broadcast media, and most recently, digital media. That much is uncontroversial. The suitability of that model for new media is much more controversial.

Two examples from the music industry make this point. The first is the dispute between the Recording Industry Association of America (RIAA) and the Internet firm Napster involving Napster's failure to pay royalties on music downloaded by fans. In addition to losses sustained by record companies, this case also involves a loss of command over the musical product by artists wishing to control dissemination of their work. In the second example, the recording industry has tried to argue that sound recordings should be considered "works for hire" and thus subject to a copyright term of 95 years (as opposed to the 35-year term that obtains if musicians are legally judged to be the authors of their works) (Pareles, 2000). The financial motive for this effort is that recent technological changes are making many older recordings more profitable than new releases. The legal success of these cases so far has been mixed (Hamilton, 2000).

We suspect that this juxtaposition of new technology and intellectual property law will present similar problems in the near future for composers, choreographers, and playwrights.

FUTURE ISSUES

Two key issues stand out for the future. The first follows directly from the trends just described: the difficulties of a professional career path in the arts may drive more talented artists to choose amateur involvement. As superstar markets become more pervasive—driving some wages up, but most down—and the supply of artists outstrips demand at least at the top professional level, we envision potential professionals with more reasons to choose the avocational route (albeit, perhaps, after or because of an unsuccessful try at the professional world), and consequently a greater role for serious aficionados and semiprofessional performers.

Second, the next chapter points to changes in the demography of arts organizations that may reduce the opportunities for artists to gain professional experience and mature in their careers. Midsized nonprofit organizations, in particular, appear to be facing more serious financial pressures than either large or small organizations. If some of these organizations disappear, a vital training ground for actors, ballet dancers, opera singers, and classical musicians will also get smaller. In this case, graduates of the conservatory may be forced to choose between taking a job in the "low-end" professional sector, where standards of production are far less professional, or switching careers and participating in their art as nonprofessionals.

Chapter Six

CHARACTERISTICS OF PERFORMING ARTS ORGANIZATIONS

As we observed in Chapter Four, shifts in the demographic composition and leisure time preferences of Americans are changing the types of art that audiences most care about and the ways they wish to experience it. In the market for artists, although the superstar phenomenon is of long-standing duration, the gulf between the small group of extravagantly well-paid celebrity artists and the much larger pool of professionally trained but frequently unemployed artists appears to be widening.

This chapter examines the various types of organizations that decide what art gets produced, how it is produced, and by whom, thereby determining the supply of the performing arts delivered to audiences and the supply of jobs for artists.[1] We demonstrate that arts organizations range widely in terms of size, artistic and financial objectives, and the function they serve in bringing both the live arts and the recorded arts to the public. After a brief introduction to key organizational types and the data available to analyze them, we offer a snapshot of performing arts organizations in America as they look today to answer the following questions:

- How many performing arts organizations are there, and in which market sectors do they operate?

- What do U.S. performing arts organizations look like in terms of discipline, geographic location, size, and function within the arts delivery system?

Then we describe the key trends that have been altering these characteristics and their implications for the future.

---

[1]Although creative artists are, by definition, central to the creation of the performing arts, they generally play a very small role in determining what art actually reaches audiences.

KEY CONCEPTS

Arts organizations serve as key links in the chain that brings created works of art to audiences. As illustrated in Figure 6.1, they perform, present, reproduce, and distribute the work of art to audiences. Performers, like creators, are at the core of the creative process, providing content to presenters and reproducers. Distributors take recorded-art content and deliver it to consumers; for simplicity we include broadcasters in this category, as well as wholesale distributors and retailers. Performing and presenting organizations represent the "live" segment and reproducers and distributors represent the "recorded" segment of the delivery system.[2] The numbered hexagons represent additional organizations that act primarily as brokers: Hexagon 1 represents such organizations as music publishing companies; hexagons 2 and 3 represent such organizations as artists' management agencies and promoters.

To illustrate, consider the case of symphonic music. The creator of a new symphonic work, the composer, assigns his or her copyright to the music publisher, represented by hexagon 1, which makes the music available to performers in return for a royalty payment that it splits with the composer. The performer,

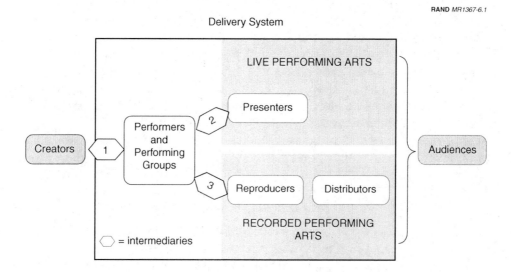

RAND *MR1367-6.1*

Figure 6.1—Organizational Structure of the Professional Performing Arts Delivery System

---

[2]For simplicity, we treat each of these roles separately, but we recognize that individuals can often serve multiple roles in the system. A choreographer, for example, may serve as the creator of a dance and also perform in the dance, and may also be the presenter.

a symphony orchestra, performs the work in the local symphony hall or performing arts center. If the orchestra owns or leases its local performance venue, it acts as both performer and presenter for its hometown performances. In addition, the orchestra may hire a promoter, represented by hexagon 2, who sets up a concert tour with presenters at selected performance venues in other cities, states, or countries. The box office receipts from touring are split between presenter, promoter, orchestra, and composer.

If the orchestra has a national (or more likely international) reputation, it may also sign a contract with a reproducer, the record company, to record the new symphonic work. A management agency, represented by hexagon 3, may or may not broker this transaction. The record company, if it is a major label, owns its own recording studio, compact disc (CD) manufacturing plant, and whole-sale distribution network for classical CDs.[3] The record company markets the new release to retailers and radio broadcasters. Depending on the nature of the contracts signed along the way, any profits from CD sales may be split between retailers, record company, orchestra, music publisher, and composer. Broad-casters pay royalties on the release based on its airtime; their revenues derive from advertisers, not record companies.[4]

In the high arts, the artistic emphasis of most performers is on live perfor-mance, which also generates the bulk of their earned revenues or receipts. Not coincidentally, both the high arts and the live segment of the professional per-forming arts are dominated by nonprofit organizations, which rely on con-tributed as well as earned income to cover their costs. Although various theories seek to explain the predominance of nonprofit organizations in the live per-forming high arts (see, for example, Throsby and Withers, 1979; Hansmann, 1981; and DiMaggio, 1982 and 1984), most are consistent with Baumol and Bowen's 1966 argument that the audiences are too small and fixed costs too high for professional live performances of ballet, opera, and symphonic music to pay their own way. In fact, with the possible exception of theater, there is considerable evidence that professional live performance of the popular arts also fails to pay its own way. In popular music, for example, live concert tours are generally loss leaders designed to leverage sales of recorded music and licensed merchandise (Vogel, 1998).[5]

---

[3]Other recorded music formats include vinyl records and audio cassette tapes, but CDs now ac-count for almost 90 percent of recording sales. The newest music media formats, digital audio discs and super audio CDs, have yet to achieve wide consumer acceptance (RIAA, 2001).

[4]For nonprofit broadcasters, sources of revenue are primarily sponsors and contributors.

[5]Professional for-profit theater is itself a highly cyclical industry, and there have been frequent pe-riods in which Broadway barely appears to have survived financially. See, for example, Baumol and Bowen (1966), Moore (1968), and NEA (1981).

In the popular arts, the artistic emphasis and bulk of earned revenues for performers are the reverse of what they are in the high arts. Most organizations are for-profit, recorded products generate the bulk of receipts, and the artistic emphasis is on the recorded product. In fact, the term "popular" sometimes appears to be synonymous with "recorded": one rarely hears reference to "popular dance" or "popular theater," neither of which has an extensive portfolio of recorded products.[6,7] The artistic emphasis on the recorded product is illustrated by popular music genres such as progressive rock and hip-hop, where the recording studio has become an extension of the musician's art (Miller and Boar, 1981; Frith, 1986). An exception might be jazz, in which the artistry still seems to be most fully expressed in live performance; interestingly, jazz is often put forward for "high art" status. Regardless of artistic emphasis, however, the data and analysis on performers in the popular as well as the high arts generally place them within the live and not the recorded segment of the delivery system. In the discussion that follows, therefore, the terms "performers" and "live performers" are used interchangeably.

Not all of the elements of the delivery system are necessarily group organizations per se; the category "performers," for example, includes individual performing artists as well as performing companies. Further, as our symphonic music illustration shows, a high degree of integration between elements is possible. Creative artists and performing artists may be the same person or persons, performers may also be presenters, and audiences may themselves participate in making art as performers or creators. Promoters may also be presenters, and, as described above, a single integrated record company may control talent scouts, recording studios, manufacturing operations, and record distribution—although not usually retailing.[8]

Understanding the organizational structure of the delivery system depicted in Figure 6.1 helps to illuminate several important conceptual reasons why apparently simple questions such as "How many performing arts organizations are there?" are in practice difficult to answer. One of the most important reasons is that, in contrast to products like automobiles, the "products" of the performing arts are extremely heterogeneous—especially when both the live and recorded segments of the delivery system are considered. Whereas the vast majority of

---

[6]We draw a distinction between popular art, which is defined to have mass commercial appeal and is generally produced in the for-profit sector, and folk art, which tends to be produced by volunteer-sector organizations in live performance.

[7]Although narrative film could arguably be considered a form of recorded theater, it is generally classified as its own art form distinct from theater. In the case of dance, the portfolio of recorded products seems to be growing: For example, the popularity of the stage show *Riverdance*, featuring Irish hard-shoe dancing, has stimulated the production of a series of very successful CDs and dance videos.

[8]See, for example, Hirsch (1990).

automobiles have four wheels, an engine, and are purchased by consumers on showroom floors, a symphonic music product, as illustrated above, may be a concert performance presented to a live audience; a concert performance broadcast over radio, television, or the Internet; a CD or audio cassette tape sold to consumers for home use; or a CD or tape broadcast over radio, television, or the Internet. Thus, in contrast to the firms that manufacture and distribute automobiles, the firms that produce these different symphonic music products fit not only within different industrial classifications, but also within entirely different production classifications.[9] The profound differences across firms in both production technologies and industrial organization make it difficult to combine the highly fragmented data on arts organizations into an overall picture.

A related conceptual issue surrounding the arts delivery system is how to define an arts organization. While it seems clear that performers such as ballet or opera companies should be considered arts organizations, as we move further toward audiences in Figure 6.1, the connection between what the organization actually does and "making art" becomes increasingly tenuous. Are distributors of videotapes and CDs really "arts organizations"? Not in the sense of making art. Nevertheless, these types of organizations are vital links in the organizational chain bringing dance, music, opera, and theater to many people who rarely, if ever, attend live events. Any broad analysis of the performing arts world must consider the role of distributors, if only to understand how new technologies such as the Internet are dramatically changing who the distributors are, what they do, and which audiences they serve.

A third issue in the analysis of the performing arts is that the performing arts industry, like the health and education industries, is made up of organizations that have, at least superficially, extremely different goals and objectives. In the auto industry, to use our previous example, the principal objective of every firm is to be profitable. This is also the principal objective of the taxable for-profit firms in the performing arts industry. It is not, however, the principal objective of the many nonprofit and volunteer-sector organizations in the performing arts, which, as we noted above, mostly operate in the live-arts segment of the delivery system. The primary operational goals of these organizations may be artistic excellence, artistic innovation, recognition and prestige, maximum audience size, maximum audience diversity, or maximum community participation. Thus while financial, employment, and output measures are adequate for

---

[9]In fact, the distinction between firms in the performing arts based on tax status (nonprofit or tax-exempt versus for-profit or taxable) is less of a barrier to many types of analysis than the second distinction, based on product characteristics (for instance, manufactured good versus service).

most analyses of the auto or entertainment industry, analyses of the performing arts world require data that are considerably more detailed.

In order to assess the implications of organizational change in the nonprofit performing arts sector, ideally we would want to know something about the missions, programming, and primary audiences of the organizations involved, as well as having data on their finances, employment, and output. In fact, although it is still not enough, we do know considerably more about arts activity that takes place within the nonprofit sector than we do about activity in the for-profit sector.[10] Unfortunately this means we know less about certain art forms—such as jazz—that tend to be performed by unaffiliated individuals or for-profit organizations than we do about other art forms—such as opera—that are dominated by nonprofit groups. We know even less about other performing arts—such as folk music and dance—that are often practiced outside formal markets in the volunteer sector.

SOURCES OF DATA

Besides financial data, which we discuss in the next chapter, there are three types of data on the characteristics of performing arts organizations:

* data on the number and disciplinary focus of organizations

* data on output

* data on programming.

Only the first type is collected systematically and in enough detail to be useful for research purposes.

Number of Organizations and Their Disciplines

The U.S. Census Bureau's Economic Census has been counting the number of taxable and tax-exempt performing, presenting, reproducing, and distributing organizations throughout the United States every five years since 1977. Unfortunately, the sampling methodology used overrepresents large employers (firms without paid employees, for example, are not sampled) and does not include the arts activities of nonmarket or informal organizations, or the arts activities of organizations embedded within larger non-arts organizations such as

---

[10]This is because the disclosure requirements imposed by the federal government on nonprofit organizations are far more comprehensive than the requirements imposed on for-profits.

universities and local governments.[11] Because so much live performing and presenting activity seems to occur within the volunteer sector, performers and presenters are more likely than reproducers or distributors to be undercounted by the Economic Census. As a result, the Economic Census data probably over-represent activity within traditional high art forms such as symphonic music and ballet. This is because symphony orchestras and ballet companies tend to be larger and more well-established than klezmer bands or Navajo dance troupes, which tend to fall into the volunteer sector. According to estimates by Peters and Cherbo (1998), for example, almost 90 percent of chamber music ensembles were missed by the U.S. Census Bureau's 1992 Census of Service Industries. Smith (1997) estimates that the number of uncounted nonprofits outnumbers the number that submit annual tax forms to the IRS by a factor of 8 to 1. Another problem with the Economic Census has to do with its classification system.[12] Performing organizations for certain high art forms, such as opera, are assigned data categories of their own.

But organizations that perform within popular and nontraditional artistic sub-disciplines, such as country and western and Balinese gamelan music, are lumped together in single-code categories such as "Other music." As a result, Economic Census data can be used to track the growth of opera companies from 1977 to the present, for example, but they cannot be used to track the growth of country music bands or gamelan orchestras. Even worse, many artists who have incorporated themselves but perform as individual acts are lumped together with visual and literary artists in the category "Independent artists, writers, and performers."[13] Therefore, unless explicitly defined otherwise, in the analysis that follows the term "performers" will refer to performing organizations, not individual artists who have incorporated as single proprietorships.

Problems of categorization also afflict the other functional links within the delivery system. Presenters of the live performing arts are grouped together with all "Promoters of performing arts, sports, and similar events," including those with and without their own facilities.

---

[11]Embedded organizations may or may not be counted as part of the population of arts organizations; it depends on whether the U.S. Census Bureau considers them to be a performing arts "establishment." The Census Bureau defines an establishment as a single physical location where manufacturing or a service is performed. A firm is defined as a business organization (taxable or tax-exempt) consisting of one or more establishments under common ownership or control.

[12]The North American Industrial Classification System (NAICS), adopted in the 1997 Economic Census, is a big improvement over the Standard Industrial Classification (SIC) system, which the old Census of Service Industries used from 1977 to 1992. Nevertheless, many organizations within the performing arts delivery system still do not fit well within the NAICS.

[13]Individual musical artists producing nonclassical forms are included in the category, "Other music groups and artists."

With respect to distributors, there is no way to disaggregate the production and distribution of performing arts products from the rest of their overall business activity. With respect to reproducers, there is no way to disaggregate their activities by art form, subdiscipline, or genre. So, for example, although Economic Census data may show us that the number of "integrated record production and distribution" firms (that is, record companies) is growing, we have no way of knowing what this might mean for, say, classical versus popular music.

A second source of data that identifies the number and disciplinary composition of performing arts organizations (although the data are relevant only to nonprofit arts organizations) is the Internal Revenue Service (IRS). Since the mid-1980s, the IRS has been making its Business Master File (BMF) and annual Return Transactions Files (RTFs)—more commonly known as the "Form 990 data"—available through the Urban Institute's National Center for Charitable Statistics. Both files are based on tax forms filed by tax-exempt charitable organizations. In the performing arts, the relevant organizations have Section 501(c)(3) status under the U.S. Tax Code. Unfortunately, the demise of 501(c)(3) arts organizations is rarely reflected in the BMF because organizations generally do not tell the IRS when they go out of business. As a result, the BMF tends to overstate the number of formal nonprofit performing arts organizations that actually exist. On the other hand, the Form 990 data do not capture information on arts organizations that fall below the $25,000 threshold revenue requirement for filing Form 990 each year, so they tend to understate the number of very small nonprofits operating in the volunteer sector. Neither file contains data on arts organizations that are embedded within other non-arts nonprofit organizations. Nevertheless, the annual IRS data are more timely than the five-year Economic Census data, and the IRS's adoption of the National Taxonomy of Exempt Entities (NTEE) coding scheme means that its data avoid many of the ambiguities of the NAICS with respect to performing and presenting organizations. Unfortunately, the NTEE-coded data are only available beginning in the early 1990s.[14]

Real Output

Data on the real output of the live segment of the performing arts—number of performances, number of productions, number of admissions tickets purchased, or other "product" measures—are seriously lacking. In contrast to recorded music products, for example, where Economic Census data include

---

[14]The original NTEE coding system was developed by the National Center for Charitable Statistics (NCCS) and several major nonprofit organizations during the 1980s. The IRS itself first applied the NTEE system to the BMF in 1995, but Form 990 data have been retroactively coded by NCCS back to 1992 (NCCS, 2001).

estimates of the value of all prerecorded CDs, records, and tapes that have been produced and shipped within the United States, as well as the value of those sitting in inventory, there are no census data on the total value of opera, dance, theater, or symphony orchestra performances, or on the value of seats that were available (capacity) or filled (occupancy) for each performance. The only consistent sources for output data are the NSOs and industry associations, as well as a few private organizations that regularly publish directories and periodicals containing information on individual productions and artists. Examples include *Musical America,* published by Primedia Inc., and the periodicals *Variety* and *Daily Variety,* which cover Broadway and the film industry.

Programming

Finally, with the notable exception of OPERA America, the NSOs for performing groups provide very little in the way of consistent data over time on programming. Information from the NSO for presenters is only marginally better. The lack of such data makes it extremely difficult to assess the implications of organizational changes on programming within the performing arts delivery system in any systematic way.

These holes in the data make it difficult to present an accurate and comprehensive profile of performing arts organizations in the United States. In the live arts, we cannot precisely say how many organizations there are, where they perform, or whether they are growing bigger or smaller. We do not know how many modern dance performances or jazz festivals took place in any particular year, or whether there were more or less that year than the year before. Beyond broad disciplinary categorizations, we also do not know in what ways live arts organizations may be changing their programming—for example, whether local performing arts centers are choosing to present *A Moon for the Misbegotten* more or less often than *Oklahoma!.* In the recorded arts, we often cannot isolate firms' performing arts activity from their other business activities, let alone identify activity within particular disciplinary genres over time.

Finally, it is true that all research is constrained by the sample characteristics and classification systems of the available data. But because there are so few sources for comprehensive, time-series data on performing arts organizations, broad analyses of the performing arts world are particularly constrained. In the analysis that follows, the Economic Census is often the sole source of data we can use to make comparisons across organizations that perform different functions within very different sectors of the economy. Therefore, it is important to acknowledge again the limitations imposed by this data source. It is biased toward middle- and big-budget organizations. It cannot be used to track characteristics of a fixed set of organizations over time. And it is constrained by a classification system that generally does not make distinctions beyond the major art forms such as theater and dance.

CURRENT PICTURE

In this section we analyze what the data tell us about the number, size, discipline, market sector, and geographic dispersion of arts organizations today, starting first with the performing groups and presenting organizations that provide live performances and then moving to the reproducers and distributors that provide recorded performances. Our analysis focuses on organizations that are taxable and those that have formally incorporated themselves as tax-exempt, but note that the smallest of these nonprofits actually fall within the volunteer sector, as we define it.

The Live Performing Arts

Music and Theater Companies Are Most Prevalent

How many performing organizations are there in each of the major performing arts disciplines? According to data from the 1997 Economic Census, there were over 8,000 companies that gave live performances in the United States, of which just under 40 percent were theater groups, 6 percent dance companies, 2 percent opera companies, 10 percent symphony or chamber music orchestras, and 45 percent groups performing other forms of nonclassical music.[15]

The relative proportions of live performing arts companies in the nonprofit versus for-profit sectors vary considerably by discipline, as shown in Figure 6.2. Whereas theater groups are roughly evenly split between the two sectors, the majority of dance companies and the vast majority of opera companies and classical music organizations are organized on a nonprofit basis. In contrast, the vast majority of groups and artists in the "Other music" category, that is, those who do not perform classical instrumental music, are organized as for-profits, which is consistent with the many popular music genres included within this category. (The much smaller number of nonprofit nonclassical music groups can reasonably be supposed to consist of the various choral, folk, and

---

[15]As defined by the Census Bureau, "Classical music organizations" here include symphony orchestras, chamber ensembles, and other organizations that identify themselves as producers of instrumental classical music. "Other music groups and artists" include dance or stage bands or orchestras; jazz music groups; choral music groups; and folk, rock, soul, country and western, etc., music groups—that is, all forms of music except classical instrumental music. For simplicity, we use the term "classical" to refer to classical instrumental music.

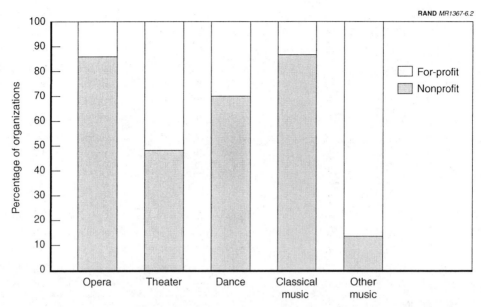

RAND *MR1367-6.2*

SOURCE: U.S. Bureau of the Census, 1997 Economic Census.

**Figure 6.2—Proportion of Nonprofit and For-Profit Performing Companies
by Discipline, 1997**

ethnic music performers that also make up the potpourri of musical genres included within this category.)

In fact, because there are many more for-profit "other music" performers than
there are nonprofit classical music organizations, if all musical forms are combined under the single category "music," the for-profit groups outnumber the
nonprofits 3 to 1. Of course, none of these comparisons takes into account the
activities of unincorporated performing artists and groups, for which we have
no data but which we believe to be considerable. It is impossible to know
whether there are relatively more of these groups within dance, theater, opera,
classical music, or nonclassical music.

Most Performing Groups Are Small

As shown in Figure 6.3, the average revenues of live performing arts organizations vary somewhat both by discipline and sector. Regardless of discipline or
sector, however, most organizations are small. In theater, dance, and classical
music, for example, approximately 60 to 75 percent of the live performing
groups that operated year-round had revenues of less than $500,000 in 1997. A
notable exception is opera, where over 60 percent of nonprofit organizations

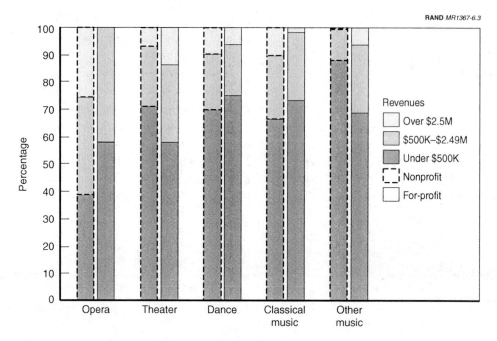

SOURCE: U.S. Bureau of the Census, 1997 Economic Census.

Figure 6.3—Percentage of Nonprofit and For-Profit Performing Groups Within Revenue Classes, 1997

had revenues greater than $500,000, and almost 30 percent had revenues greater than $2.5 million. This is probably due to the generally higher fixed costs of putting on an opera, which consequently require a higher matching revenue stream. In opera, as in dance and classical music (but not theater or "other music"), for-profit performers tended to be smaller than nonprofit organizations.

This may be because, in contrast to nonprofit performers who receive grants and contributions, for-profit performers must rely primarily on box office receipts from the relatively small audiences for these art forms.

The Market Concentration of Performing Companies Is Not High

As we might expect based on the large number of small-budget performing organizations, the level of market concentration among most kinds of performing groups is not high relative to other industries, including—as we shall see—the recorded segment of the performing arts. As shown in Table 6.1, opera, with the highest average revenues and presumably the highest fixed costs of the four art forms represented in Economic Census data, also has the most concentrated industry structure. This is consistent with mainstream economic theories about

Table 6.1

Total Revenues and Percentage of Revenues Held by the 4 Largest and the
20 Largest Performing Companies, 1997

	Total Revenues ($1,000s)	4 largest companies		20 largest companies	
		Nonprofits (percent)	For-profits (percent)	Nonprofits (percent)	For-profits (percent)
Opera	593,608[a]	53.4	—[a]	80.4	—[a]
Theater[b]	3,225,537	3.3	9.2	9.9	25.2
Dance	432,690	16.7	11.8	38.6	20.2
Classical music	1,078,228	18.0	0.9	50.3	2.3
Other music	2,248,281	0.6	5.0	1.8	15.3

SOURCE: U.S. Bureau of the Census, 1997 Economic Census.
[a]For-profit data withheld to avoid disclosing data for individual companies.
[b]Does not include dinner theaters.

the relationship between fixed costs and industry structure: The higher the fixed costs, the more difficult it is for new firms to enter the industry and take revenues away from existing firms. The four largest opera companies, all nonprofits, received over half of the total revenues earned by nonprofit opera companies.

The least concentrated industry was "Other music," where the top four for-profit groups earned just 5 percent, and the top four nonprofit groups less than 1 percent, of combined nonprofit and for-profit revenues. This suggests very low barriers to entry into the field of nonclassical music, which plausibly translates into both a diversity of musical forms and competitive prices for musical performances. In fact, taken as a whole, the Economic Census data support other, anecdotal data that paint a dynamic picture of the nonclassical music field in which specialized small, for-profit, and volunteer-sector musical groups are reaching out to attract new audiences and new participants

Geographic Counts of Performing Groups Are Not Good Measures of Access to the Arts

One of the most important issues in the organizational demography of the performing arts is whether potential audiences have access to live performances of theater, dance, opera, and music. A frequently voiced concern is that Americans living in small towns and rural areas have less access to the live arts than Americans in urban centers. To explore this issue, a common approach is to conduct geographic counts of performing organizations. However, as we argue below, such counts are not good measures of access to the arts.

Census data indicate that California and New York dominate the rest of the country in terms of total numbers of nonprofit and for-profit performing organizations and in terms of these organizations' revenues and receipts. However, because California and New York are also the first and third most populous states in the country, respectively, we would expect to find a preponderance of performing groups in these two states. Another and perhaps more appropriate measure of the relative access that residents of different states have to the live performing arts is the number of performing establishments per capita. Measured this way, the story is quite different. In per capita terms, the District of Columbia had by far the greatest concentration of nonprofit performing organizations, with 45 groups per million inhabitants; and Mississippi had the least, with just 6 groups per million inhabitants. On the for-profit side, Nevada dominates all others with 77 taxable performing acts per million inhabitants, while North Dakota comes in last with fewer than 2 groups per million inhabitants.

Even when expressed in terms of groups per capita, however, these numbers provide only a very rough guide to the geographic distribution of access to the live performing arts, for two reasons. First, residence within a state does not necessarily reflect geographic proximity to its live performing arts activity. For example, residents of northwestern Nevada do not necessarily benefit from that state's abundance of for-profit performing organizations, which are heavily concentrated in Las Vegas. Similarly, residents of Southwestern Mississippi may well find it easier to access the theaters and jazz clubs of New Orleans than residents of northwestern Louisiana, whose closest cultural center is probably Dallas.

The second reason why the number of performing groups per capita is a very rough measure of access is touring. In principle, touring could serve an important role in providing access to small and geographically isolated communities that cannot support their own performing companies—as it historically has done. However, it could also simply serve to rotate performing groups through a set of communities that are already well-served at home. Unfortunately, Census data provide no information on the number of performing groups that tour, the share of revenues derived from touring, or the geographic distribution of tours, and so cannot be used to distinguish between these two alternatives.

Nonprofit Presenters, Key to Access, Are Located Throughout the Country

Another way to consider the question of access is to focus on the organizations that present the performing arts before live audiences. In fact, leaving aside the question of touring, it is important to know who the presenters are and where they are located, because many of the performing organizations described above do not operate their own presentation facilities. It takes presenters as well as performers to deliver live art to audiences.

According to the 1997 Economic Census, about 1,000 U.S. promoters operated performing arts, sports, or other recreational facilities as independent establishments in 1997, just under 400 of which were nonprofit. Unfortunately, the Census data do not allow us to distinguish between performing arts venues and other types of recreational facilities—but in any case the distinction may not be important because many of these facilities are used for varied events. On net, however, the Census data almost certainly greatly underrepresent total numbers of live performing arts presenters, because so many of them are embedded within state and local governments or educational institutions.

A better source of data on arts presenters in the United States is the Association of Performing Arts Presenters (APAP), which as of 1999 put its membership at roughly 1,600. According to a 1993 membership survey (APAP, 1995), approximately 46 percent of respondents were independent nonprofit organizations, while another 38 percent were public or private educational institutions. Just 1.2 percent of respondents were commercial for-profit organizations; a tiny 0.6 percent were unincorporated. Note, however, that the APAP membership may not be representative of all presenters—for example, for-profit theater houses such as the Shubert and Jujamcyn chains are not members of APAP—so these numbers probably overestimate the relative proportion of nonprofit to for-profit organizations.

Interestingly, the geographic distribution of arts presenters revealed by the survey is fairly even. Equal numbers of respondents were located in small cities and large urban areas (36 percent), with smaller numbers located in rural areas (16 percent) and suburban areas (12 percent). The top three states represented were California, New York, and Ohio, but regional disparities, when controlled for population, were surprisingly low. This may reflect state and local government policies that have broadened access to the arts by supporting the creation of performing arts centers in regional hubs, small towns, and suburban neighborhoods across the country. It also reflects the important role played by highly geographically dispersed educational institutions in sponsoring and presenting the live performing arts.

Educational Institutions Are the Most Common Type of Presenter

Table 6.2, which offers a look at who the presenters are in terms of their organizational type rather than their tax status, shows that educational institutions are the most prevalent organizational type (37 percent). Arts and civic centers (13 percent) and local arts agencies (7 percent) are also well-represented in the APAP membership.

The large number of presenters connected to educational institutions suggests that the policies of colleges and universities may strongly influence the ability of live performing organizations to reach audiences. Many of the decisions about what gets performed and who performs it are being made by institutions that do not consider the performing arts central to their mission. In fact, more than 40 percent of the survey respondents did not consider presenting arts programs

Table 6.2

Membership of APAP by Category of Presenting Organization, 1993

	Number	Percent
Educational institutions	188	37
Public or private college or university	179	36
School or school district	9	1
Performing arts facilities	145	28
Performance facility	69	14
Arts or civic center	68	13
Culturally specific center	8	1
Cultural series organizations	63	13
Festival, fair, or cultural series	60	13
Culturally specific arts organization	3	0
Local arts agency	36	7
Performing group/producer	11	2
Museum, gallery, or library	7	2
Other[a]	52	10
TOTAL	502	100

SOURCE: Association of Performing Arts Presenters (1995).

NOTE: Percentages do not sum to 100 because some organizations are included in multiple categories.

[a]The category "Other" includes religious, business, union, and state and federal government organizations.

to be central to their mission; rather, they considered the arts either distinct from or complementary to another mission. Many in this group were college and university presenters.

Music and Dance Programs Are Most Likely To Be Presented

In terms of programming activity, music, dance, theater, and opera/musical theater programs were most often reported by respondents to the APAP survey (see Figure 6.4). Musical programs were reported by 89 percent of respondents, 76 percent reported dance programs, 71 percent reported theater programs, and 53 percent reported opera or musical theater programs. In terms of programming within art forms, popular genres such as rock and roll and jazz dominated musical programming, while modern and folk dance presentations dominated dance programming. Interestingly, the survey suggests that ballet is relatively more likely to be presented in small cities and rural areas, while the reverse is true for modern dance. APAP (1995) explains this in terms of competition, arguing that urban areas are more likely to have their own professional ballet companies.[16]

---

[16]But urban areas are also more likely to have their own modern dance companies. An alternative explanation is that ballet is preferred to modern dance in more conservative rural communities. Relevant empirical evidence for this explanation, applied to opera, is presented in Pierce (2000).

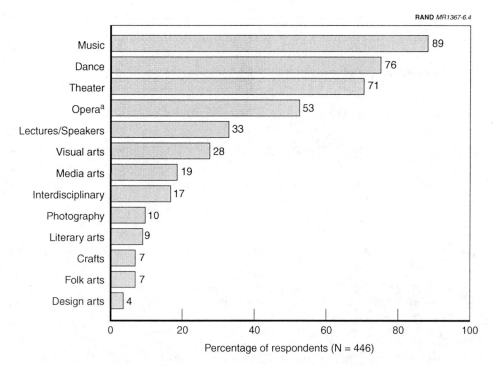

SOURCE: Association of Performing Arts Presenters, 1995.
[a]Includes musical theater.

Figure 6.4—Arts Presenters' Programming Activity by Discipline, 1993

The Recorded Performing Arts

We know far less about firms that produce and distribute the recorded performing arts (a category that includes broadcast live arts) than we do about firms
that perform and present live performing arts, for the reasons described above.
However, based on definitions provided by the Census Bureau, we can identify
four categories of organizations relevant to the production and distribution of
the recorded performing arts:[17]

- firms primarily engaged in producing and distributing musical recordings,
  in publishing music, or in providing sound recording and related services

----

[17]Classification and definitions are based on the North American Industrial Classification System
(NAICS), which is used in the 1997 Economic Census. A large category we do not consider here is
motion picture and video production and distribution, but (as noted above) we do not analyze the
film industry here. The manufacture and distribution of musical instruments is also outside the
scope of this analysis.

- firms that operate radio or television studios and facilities for the programming and transmission of programming to the public, as well as data on establishments that assemble television program material and transmit it over cable or satellite systems

- firms primarily engaged in the wholesale distribution of prerecorded CDs, audio or video tapes, and phonograph records

- firms primarily engaged in retailing new prerecorded audio and video tapes, CDs, and phonograph records.

Most Recorded Arts Organizations Are For-Profit

By far the majority of organizations that produce and distribute the recorded performing arts are taxable. The 1997 Economic Census does not publish information about nonprofit organizations within any of the classifications listed above, but, for broadcasting at least, we can estimate the number of nonprofit organizations on the basis of IRS data.[18] As shown in Table 6.3, less than 20 percent of broadcasting organizations were in the nonprofit sector.

Recorded Arts Firms Are Concentrated in New York and California

Geographically, the recording and broadcasting industries, like the live performing arts, are heavily concentrated in New York and Los Angeles, with a much smaller center of activity in Nashville, Tennessee. However, because the distribution networks for the products of these industries are nationwide, production location has very little effect on the geographic distribution of consumers. At least in urban areas, consumers in Hawaii and Florida have as much access to CDs and television programming as consumers in California or New

Table 6.3

Numbers of Recorded Arts Organizations by Activity, 1997

	Number of For-profits	Number of Nonprofits
Music recording and publishing	2,935	NA
Broadcasting	8,789	1,549
Music wholesalers	1,418	NA
Music stores	8,158	NA

SOURCES: U.S. Bureau of the Census, 1997 Economic Census and National Center for Charitable Statistics, 1998 Core File.

---

[18]These data are taken from Form 990s filed by nonprofit 501(c)(3) organizations with annual revenues greater than $25,000. In radio, for example, they therefore include most National Public Radio affiliates, but do not include the student-run station at the local university.

York.[19] This is in contrast to the live performing arts, where production must occur in front of the audience, so that audience penetration is inversely correlated with geographic distance from production location. Further, as recorded arts products become smaller and more transportable and digital technologies allow consumers to share content across a growing variety of media devices, the locational freedom offered by the recorded arts is in growing contrast to the locational constraints of the live arts.

Industry Concentration in the Recorded Arts Is High

What could be more of an issue—and possibly a concern—is the high degree of industry concentration in the recording, music publishing, and television and cable broadcasting industries, suggesting that entry barriers are high and competition may be limited.[20] Almost half of the total income earned by television producers, for example, reflects the earnings of just four very large firms (Table 6.4). Similarly, four firms earned fully two-thirds of the total receipts of all integrated record producers and distributors in 1997, and 20 firms accounted for almost 100 percent of the total.[21] In May 2000, the U.S. Federal Trade Commission (FTC) reached an antitrust settlement with the five largest record companies—representing approximately 85 percent of all U.S. CD

Table 6.4

Percentage of Receipts by Largest Recorded Performing Arts Firms, 1997

	Total receipts ($1,000s)	4 largest firms (percent)	20 largest firms (percent)
Sound recording			
Record production only	182,369	20.4	48.1
Integrated record production and distribution	8,735,863	66.9	96.8
Music publishing	1,368,407	48.5	73.0
Recording studios	540,601	6.9	20.5
Broadcasting			
Radio broadcasting	10,648,134	22.7	42.2
Television broadcasting	29,777,076	48.6	71.3
Cable distribution	45,389,578	42.3	74.3

SOURCE: U.S. Bureau of the Census, 1997 Economic Census.

---

[19]In broadcasting there is still some issue about the influence of production location on programming (New York–based television producers may be more likely to showcase New York–based artists and companies, for example) but as long as the industry is competitive, producers must be at least somewhat responsive to their national consumer audience in order to stay profitable.

[20]It is also worth noting that there has been considerable consolidation within these industries both nationally and internationally since the 1997 Economic Census was conducted.

[21]More detailed analyses of the structure of the American popular music industry can be found in Sanjek and Sanjek (1991); Scott (1999) discusses why companies in the music business tend to cluster together.

sales—ordering them to discontinue their practice of coercing potential discounters into maintaining minimum advertised prices for CDs (FTC, 2000). But more than high prices, the concern is that concentration in the recorded arts industry will limit innovation. Some studies have found this to be true in the past (Peterson and Berger, 1996).

To summarize our points about the current picture of performing arts organizations: As of the late 1990s, available data suggest that the live performing groups in the high arts are overwhelmingly organized as nonprofit organizations, whereas groups that perform popular music are overwhelmingly for-profit. Performers are geographically concentrated in New York and California, but less so than the relative size of the populations of these two states might predict. Most performing organizations are small in terms of their revenues, and many rely primarily on voluntary labor from their communities, defining them as volunteer-sector organizations. With the exception of opera, the barriers to entry for new firms are not terribly high. Presenting organizations also operate primarily in the nonprofit sector, but a large fraction of them are embedded within higher education institutions. In contrast, the recorded arts are overwhelmingly for-profit, and are heavily concentrated both geographically and in terms of revenues.

KEY TRENDS

The Average Nonprofit Performing Group Is Getting Smaller; the Average For-Profit Is Getting Bigger

Over the past two decades, the number of live performing organizations has grown significantly but their average revenues—at least in the nonprofit sector—have not. As shown in Figure 6.5, the number of both nonprofit and for-profit performing groups increased between 1982 and 1997, but at very different rates. Whereas the number of for-profit performers expanded by 44 percent over the 15-year period (an annual average increase of 3 percent), the number of nonprofit performers increased approximately twice as fast (an annual average increase of 6 percent). During this same period, the average revenue of for-profits measured in 1992 dollars grew by 13 percent (an annual average increase of less than 1 percent), while average real revenues of nonprofits actually fell by 7 percent (an annual average decline of 0.5 percent).

Because Census data over time represent a changing sample of performing organizations, it is impossible to know whether declines in average revenues calculated from Census data imply declines for existing nonprofits or whether they reflect the entrance of many smaller groups into the nonprofit live performing arts. Regardless, in aggregate terms the trend has been toward more but smaller

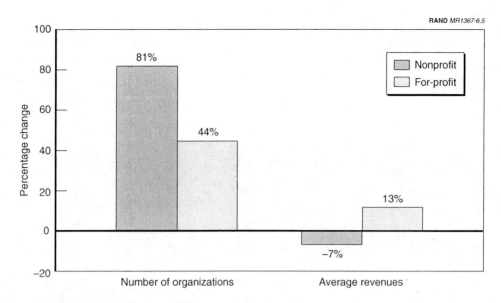

SOURCE: U.S. Census Bureau, 1982 and 1997.

**Figure 6.5—Changes in the Number and Revenue Size of
Performing Organizations, 1982–1997**

nonprofits and more but larger for-profits.[22] Thus the relatively unconcentrated nonprofit sector is becoming even less concentrated, while the already concentrated for-profit sector is becoming more so.

Patterns of Growth Differ by Sector and Discipline

Annual growth rates in numbers of organizations disguise a variety of experiences across disciplines over the 1982–1997 period, most evident in the category "other music," where the number of nonprofit performers shot up by over 9 percent (Figure 6.6). Increases in the numbers of nonprofit theater, dance, opera, and classical music performers were also significant, but less pronounced, ranging between 4.5 and 6 percent. On the for-profit side, there were fewer new organizations overall. The slow growth in the number of commercial dance groups is noticeable, but there were very few to begin with.

_____

[22]It is possible that some or even all of the apparent trend in number and average size of revenues of live performing arts nonprofits between 1982 and 1997 can be explained by improvements in the Census Bureau's ability to identify small nonprofit arts organizations. However, this would not explain why the average real revenue for the growing number of for-profits is increasing.

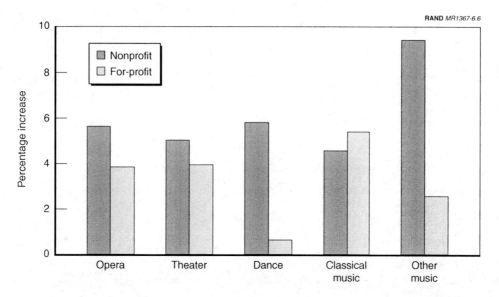

SOURCE: U.S. Census Bureau, 1998 Economic Census and 1982 Census of Service Industries.

**Figure 6.6—Annual Increases in Numbers of Performing Organizations
by Discipline, 1982–1997**

In terms of real revenue growth, illustrated in Figure 6.7, the fastest growing nonprofit category was opera, averaging almost 2 percent per year per company. By the standards of most established industries, this was a healthy growth rate, confirming those who have claimed the existence of an "opera boom" over the past 15 years.[23] The discipline with the greatest decline was "other music," which fell almost 4 percent per year per performing group. The extremely strong growth in the number of nonprofit performing organizations, combined with declining budgets particularly in nonclassical music categories, may suggest a new trend in the organizational dynamics of the performing arts world: a proliferation of niche-market performers within the volunteer sector who have either just come into existence or had been previously operating unseen because they were unincorporated.

In the for-profit sector only two of the disciplines actually experienced real revenue growth between 1982 and 1997: dance and nonclassical music. Of these, the more significant is the growth in average revenues of firms performing

---

[23]Unfortunately, opera data are not available for the for-profit sector because of Census Bureau rules against disclosure of proprietary information.

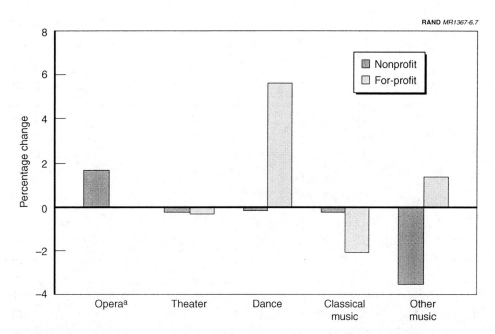

SOURCE: U.S. Census Bureau, 1998 Economic Census and 1982 Census of Service Industries.

aData not available for the for-profit sector.

Figure 6.7—Annual Change in Average Total Revenues for Performing Groups by Discipline, 1982–1997

nonclassical music, which increased at a rate of 1.4 percent.[24] As we noted above, the many musical groups within this category perform popular genres like rock, soul, and country and western, which appeal to a large and diversified audience. If these popular music firms are excluded from the for-profit total, the average change becomes negative (–0.3 percent) and the for-profit sector looks more like the nonprofit sector.

Nonprofit Performing Arts Venues Are Proliferating

Although consistent data over time on presenting organizations are lacking, formal and anecdotal evidence suggests that performing arts venues proliferated in the 1970s, 1980s, and 1990s, especially in the nonprofit sector. For example, 1993 APAP data indicate that over one-third of all existing venues were

_____

[24]This is because, as noted above, the number of for-profit dance groups is very small.

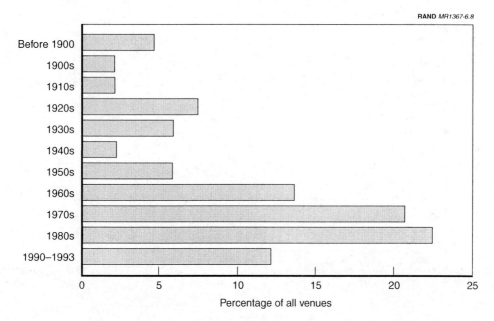

SOURCE: Association of Performing Arts Presenters.

Figure 6.8—Establishment of Performing Venues by Decade, as of 1993

built between 1980 and 1993 (Figure 6.8). One reason for the large numbers of venues built in recent years may be the growing emphasis placed by local and state governments, which are the major financers of many of these performance venues, on the economic benefits of the arts. Community development block grants, for example, are being used to finance the building of theaters, symphony halls, and all-purpose performing arts centers (Larson, 1997). Many of these newer facilities may be replacements for older facilities that have fallen into disrepair through the years.

FUTURE ISSUES

The data on organizations within the performing arts delivery system, although imperfect, not only characterize those organizations in terms of how many there are, how big they are, and what they do, they also point to what the delivery system may look like in the future. These data, combined with case study evidence and popular press accounts, suggest four trends that are particularly worth noticing.

Dynamism of Small, Volunteer-Sector Performers

The rapid growth of small, nonprofit, nonprofessional performing groups in all fields except opera suggests the growing vitality of community-based performing arts in America. These groups, many of which have revenues well under $100,000, tend to emphasize local participation and rely heavily on volunteer labor provided by local artists and administrators. Some are brand-new organizations, but others may have only recently incorporated as 501(c)(3) organizations, and so are only now being included in official statistics. Almost by definition, these groups do not feature big-budget productions or celebrity artists.

Music is the only discipline for which the data distinguish between high (classical) and popular or folk genres. Data from the "other music" category of the Economic Census suggest that many of the small musical groups that are proliferating do not perform classical music. Anecdotal evidence also suggests a high degree of nonclassical programming among other small performing arts groups. According to data collected by the research firm NuStats, almost 50 percent of organizations involved in folk arts activities had annual budgets under $100,000, and fully one-third had budgets under $50,000 (Peterson, 1996).

Rapid Growth of the Performing Arts Infrastructure

The large number of new performance venues reported by APAP membership indicates that the performing arts infrastructure is still growing rapidly. But who will use these facilities? Many of the government-sponsored venues, for example, are built with the expressed purpose of providing space for small arts groups to perform but, ironically, many small groups cannot perform there because the facilities were established as union houses and these low-budget groups cannot afford to pay union wages.[25] In addition, once these facilities are built, will they be able to afford their day-to-day operating costs? We touch upon this question in the next chapter.

Increasing Concentration of the Recorded Arts

The for-profit music and broadcasting industries are among the most concentrated U.S. industries, and increasingly they are merging with each other. For recorded music, concentration is on a global scale: Of the current top four major record labels (in 1999 there were six), just one is an American company.

---

[25]We are indebted to Ben Cameron, Executive Director, Theatre Communications Group, for pointing this out. For a fuller discussion of the role that unions play in the performing arts, see Caves (2000).

Many analysts believe even more consolidation is in store, as the four majors continue to buy up midsized independents (Pollack, 2000).

What will this mean for consumers? No one knows for sure, and the growing role of the Internet makes forecasting even more difficult. But past research on the music business suggests there is an inverse relationship between the diversity of popular music offerings and the degree of corporate concentration in the industry (Peterson and Berger, 1990, 1996). To the extent that this type of consolidation limits competition and consumer choice, it is likely to raise antitrust issues for the commercial music sector.

Impact of the Internet

While increased concentration of the recorded arts industry could imply less choice and higher prices for consumers, in music (and soon maybe in other performing art forms as well) this tendency may be offset by musicians' and consumers' use of the Internet. Popular press accounts suggest that the Internet is allowing both musicians and consumers to circumvent the record company "gatekeepers" that have largely controlled access to music in the past. One possible implication of the decline in importance of record company gatekeepers is an increase in the influence of web-based critics who may or may not be independent of the record companies.

More immediately, while press accounts suggest record companies are coming to terms with music distribution over the Internet, independent distributors and retailers of recorded music are losing out (Stroud, 2000). Recent legal actions seem likely to do little to prevent these organizations from hemorrhaging even more money. Will "bricks-and-mortar" music retailers go the way of the dodo? If so, what will it mean for consumers who are on the wrong side of the digital divide?

Web-based technologies are also allowing once geographically restricted forms of art to reach new and far-flung audiences. For musical groups, the benefits of the Internet are particularly strong, because it allows audiences to actually listen to their work and potentially even to buy it. But even for dance and theater groups, the Internet can be an important clearinghouse, allowing them to communicate with potential audiences and helping to create a community of support. Thus, at least potentially, the Internet is creating profitable opportunities for small, niche-market for-profit arts organizations that had previously been dependent upon their local ethnic and cultural communities for support.

Chapter Seven

FINANCIAL SITUATION OF PERFORMING ARTS ORGANIZATIONS

How to finance the performing arts—particularly, how to finance live performances of nonprofit theater, ballet, opera, and classical music—has been an issue for performing arts enthusiasts since at least the early 20th century. As noted in Chapter Three, by the 1920s even the wealthiest individuals were unable or unwilling to take on sole financial responsibility for such high-cost performing organizations as symphony orchestras and opera companies. This development led to the creation of today's standard model for the nonprofit organization, in which a board of directors or trustees is empowered to oversee, but not wholly support, the financial health of the institution.[1] It was not until Baumol and Bowen (1966), however, that the chronic nature of the problem professional live performing groups face in raising sufficient revenues to cover costs was widely recognized. Baumol and Bowen's work, which argued that the live performing arts, unlike the recorded popular arts, can never entirely support themselves in the marketplace, was a primary motivation for increased funding of the NEA, the increases in foundation funding that followed the Ford initiative, and, more generally, direct government funding for the arts.[2]

In the decades that followed Baumol and Bowen's work, professional nonprofit performing groups and presenters witnessed a dramatic increase both in the amounts and diversity of sources of contributed revenues. Direct federal support has been a relatively small but significant part of the funding mix, leveraging private and state and local government support for the arts through a system of matching grants and grants-in-aid to states. Recently, however, as pointed out by Cherbo and Wyszomirski (2000), this system has begun to break down. The battle over continued funding of the NEA in the early 1990s provides

---

[1]See, for example, Levine (1988).

[2]Baumol and Bowen (1966) did not distinguish between nonprofit and for-profit live performing organizations in their analysis. In fact, many of their examples are taken from the for-profit Broadway theater. Elsewhere, Baumol and Baumol implicitly argue in favor of government subsidies for Broadway (Baumol and Baumol, 1977; 1985b).

vivid evidence of the controversy over government, and especially federal government, funding of the arts.

In this chapter we take a detailed look at financing patterns in the performing arts. We concentrate our discussion on the professional nonprofit live performing arts—in part because that sector's financial problems are the subject of greatest policy concern, and in part because we have so little data on the for-profit live and recorded arts segments of the performing arts delivery system. Since voluntary-sector institutions receive most of their support in the form of volunteer labor and in-kind donations, finances have little relevance for them per se.

After a brief discussion of key concepts and data issues, we describe the aggregate financial portrait of performing arts organizations today and show how that profile varies by discipline and how it is changing. To conclude, we discuss the strategies that both for-profit and nonprofit professional organizations have been using to address their financial pressures, and we identify some of the issues these strategies raise for the future.

KEY CONCEPTS

Whether they are part of the performing arts delivery system (and whether they operate in the live or the recorded segments of that system), there are several basic differences between the finances of for-profit and nonprofit institutions. As noted in the previous chapter, commercial firms are in business to make a profit and rely for their revenues on market earnings. Nonprofit organizations, on the other hand, in exchange for tax-exempt status and its prohibition on profit distribution, are organized to collect revenues from a wide variety of earned and unearned income sources.[3]

For nonprofit as well as for-profit performing groups, earned income includes admission (box office) receipts, touring and institutional fees as well as earnings from unrelated business activities (concessions, food sales, gifts shops, etc.), and investment income.[4] For the recorded arts, product sales and advertising slots substitute for admission receipts. Unearned income to the nonprofit sector consists of grants and contributions. These unearned revenues come from a variety of sources including federal, state, and local government, foundations, individuals, and businesses.

---

[3]We use the terms "unearned" and "contributed" income interchangeably.

[4]Income from investments is often treated as a separate category because it typically represents earnings from endowment (and is thus a form of deferred charitable giving). For simplicity, we include it here as earned income and note, as we will demonstrate, that it constitutes a very small fraction of revenues.

In addition to their various forms of direct support, nonprofit organizations have two other sources of indirect support. First, like unincorporated organizations, they receive support in the form of volunteer labor and in-kind donations. Although difficult to estimate, these noncash benefits may be substantial.[5] Second, under Section 501 of the Internal Revenue Code, contributions to 501(c)(3) nonprofit institutions are tax deductible. The government contribution to the institution is therefore equal to the tax revenues forgone in the amount of the private contribution multiplied by the contributor's tax rate. Indirect subsidies of this type include federal, state, and local taxes forgone from deductions to individual and corporate income taxes, and property gifts. This form of indirect government support far exceeds the amount of direct government support to the arts.[6]

The combination of public and private support for the nonprofit sector, including the nonprofit performing arts, is a uniquely American phenomenon that can best be described as a public-private partnership (Hall, 1987). A particularly striking feature of the partnership is that the government's indirect subsidy to nonprofit institutions through the tax deductibility of contributions is targeted according to the wishes of individual donors rather than the government. With respect to the arts, this approach is in marked contrast to that of many European countries, where government-directed support for the arts is a basic tenet of public policy (Schuster, 1994).

Despite these differences in the source of their revenues, both for-profit and nonprofit institutions must, over the long run, operate within the constraints imposed by their total revenues. But whereas the expenditures of for-profit institutions are constrained by their market earnings, the expenditures of nonprofits are typically greater than their earned revenues. This difference, often referred to as the "earnings gap" (or sometimes the "income gap"), is made up by the various forms of unearned income described above.

An important conceptual issue surrounding the earnings gap of nonprofit institutions, including performing arts nonprofits, concerns the extent to which they are able to reduce their expenditures without sacrificing their basic missions. As we discuss in greater detail below, whether the problem of the earnings gap in the nonprofit performing arts is perceived to be severe depends greatly on the extent to which expenditures—and the underlying costs that drive them—are perceived to be under the control of the artistic directors and business managers of performing arts organizations. A second issue, which is primarily a data

---

[5]See, for example, Colonna (1995).

[6]Schuster et al. (1983) estimate that indirect subsidies make up two-thirds of all government support to the arts.

issue, concerns the way that the gap is reported or calculated. Since nonprofit institutions have an incentive to manipulate the size of their earnings gaps in order to motivate fundraising campaigns, accurate calculation of the gap is not always straightforward. Nonetheless, nonprofit institutions are, over the long-run, subject to the same revenue constraints as for-profit institutions in determining their total expenditures: i.e., their expenditures cannot exceed their revenues.

Finally, no analysis of the financial situation of performing arts organizations would be complete without a reference to the "cost disease," a theory put forward by Baumol and Bowen in their classic 1966 study of the economics of the performing arts. In that work, they asserted that, because dance companies, theater groups, opera companies, and orchestras cannot use technology to substitute for increasingly expensive artistic labor, over time performing groups would see their costs per unit of output rising faster than the general price level. If, furthermore, performing groups are either unable or unwilling to raise ticket prices in tandem with these rising costs, their earnings gaps must grow larger over time.

DATA SOURCES

Ideally, tracking the finances of organizations within the performing arts delivery system would require detailed information on earned revenues, unearned revenues, and expenditures. For earned revenues and expenditures, the sources are the same as those discussed in the previous chapter: the U.S. Census Bureau's Economic Census, the IRS Form 990 data on nonprofit organizations, and the information collected by various NSOs and industry associations. By and large, these sources contain considerably more information on revenues than expenditures. For unearned revenues, potential additional sources of information are the surveys conducted by The Foundation Center (on charitable giving by foundations), the AAFRC Trust for Philanthropy (on charitable giving by individuals, presented in the publication *Giving USA*), Independent Sector (for volunteering and charitable giving by individuals), Business Committee for the Arts (on charitable giving by corporations), and various publications put out by the NEA, National Association of State Arts Agencies (NASAA), and Americans for the Arts (on grants provided by various levels of government). Unfortunately, only the NEA, NASAA, and Americans for the Arts separate performing arts data from data for other art forms, so we do not use the other sources here.

Before 1997, the Economic Census provided data on revenues plus annual and first quarter payroll for performing, presenting, reproducing, and distributing organizations classified by tax status, location, and firm size. In addition to the problems noted in the previous chapter, a major problem with using Economic Census data to track organizational finances is that, before 1997, they contain no publicly available information on expenditures other than payroll expenditures.[7] This means they cannot be used to calculate a time trend of the difference between total expenditures and revenues. In addition, although the 1997 Economic Census data on performing groups and presenters include revenue breakdowns such as membership dues and fees, admissions, and shares of receipts from concessions, before 1997 the revenue data consisted only of total revenues.

The IRS Form 990 data, based on tax forms filed by nonprofit organizations organized under Section 501 of the tax code, contain annual data on earned and unearned revenues as well as limited expenditure data for nonprofits with gross receipts in excess of $25,000. The Form 990 data provide considerable detail on the various sources of revenues for nonprofits, although they do not separate government grants from private donations. Moreover, as described in Chapter Six, since the early 1990s the IRS has adopted a very useful and consistent scheme for classifying nonprofit organizations. Unfortunately, the IRS nonprofit data suffer from two big drawbacks. First, as we noted earlier, comprehensive coverage of arts organizations did not begin until the early 1990s. Second, because of their highly disaggregated nature, the data require a significant amount of processing before they are suitable for analysis.[8]

The NSOs and industry associations also collect financial information on their members. Although industry organizations for for-profit firms provide very limited expenditure data, associations of nonprofit performing and presenting firms seem to be the best source of detailed expenditure data for this sector. However, all the caveats described in the previous chapter still apply: the information collected and reported varies (often substantially) across associations; coverage is limited to member institutions, which tend to be large and well-established; data are generally not comparable over time; and published results are reported at a high level of aggregation.

---

[7]However, the Census Bureau did put together a set of special tabulations from the 1987 Census for the NEA, and some of this information is reported in Westat (1992). The 1987 total expenditures data we report here derives from this source.

[8]Data-entry errors or changes in the reporting or accounting procedures of individual organizations, for example, can dramatically change calculations based on these data. These and other Form 990 data issues are discussed in Froelich and Knoepfle (1996).

CURRENT PICTURE

The Earnings Gap Is Still Substantial

As shown in Figure 7.1, Economic Census data indicate the earnings gap for professional nonprofit performing groups is still substantial.[9] Opera companies experienced by far the largest disparity between earned income and expenses, averaging $1.6 million each in 1997, with classical music organizations a distant second, averaging under $600,000 each. Note, however, that the category of classical music includes both symphony orchestras and chamber music groups; if there were corresponding data on symphony orchestras alone we might find a much higher average earnings gap. Other music groups, which include a medley of generally small folk and popular performers from the volunteer sector, had the smallest average gaps at $78,000.

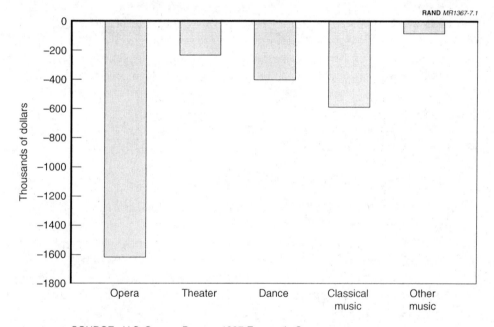

SOURCE: U.S. Census Bureau, 1997 Economic Census.

Figure 7.1—Average Earnings Gap for Nonprofit Performing Groups, 1997

[9]These data include information on some volunteer-sector groups that have formally incorporated as nonprofit organizations.

Contributed Income Has Been Making Up the Difference

Fortunately—and perhaps not coincidentally—most nonprofit performing groups have managed to make up their earnings gaps through unearned income. How important is earned income to their total budgets? As Figure 7.2 demonstrates, in 1997 it varied by discipline, ranging from well over 60 percent among nonprofit theater organizations to just over 50 percent for opera companies, symphony orchestras, and chamber ensembles. However, the earned income percentages for opera companies and classical music groups in particular reflect the income they received from endowments that benefited from the strong U.S. stock market of the 1990s. If investment income is removed from the earned income calculation, the earned income percentages for opera and classical music fall to just 44 and 45 percent, respectively.[10] This suggests that

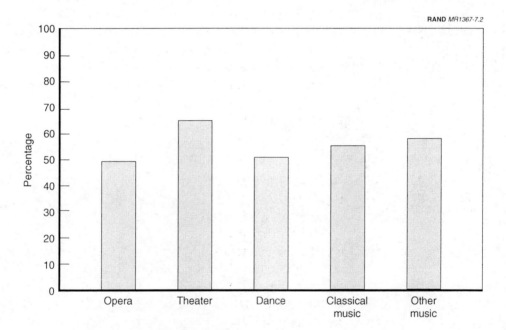

RAND MR1367-7.2

SOURCE: U.S. Census Bureau, 1997 Economic Census.

Figure 7.2—Earned Income as a Percentage of Total Revenue, 1997

_____

[10]Omitting investment income has much less impact on the earned income percentages for theater, dance, and other music companies, which fall by just 3, 1, and 1 percentage points, respectively.

these organizations may be particularly vulnerable to sudden drops in the stock and other asset markets. In any case, with or without the inclusion of investment income, these data suggest that nonprofit performing arts organizations could not operate at their current scale without generous contributions from supporters.

Where, then, do nonprofit performing groups go to make up their earnings gap? As Figure 7.3 indicates, they rely on a diverse set of sources. The most important of these are private contributions from individuals, which constitute 15 percent of total revenues. Revenues from corporate and foundation sources each represent about 7 percent of the total. Interestingly, direct government support constitutes the smallest fraction, with the NEA contributing on average just 1 percent, and other government sources (primarily state and local governments) contributing 4 percent of total revenues.

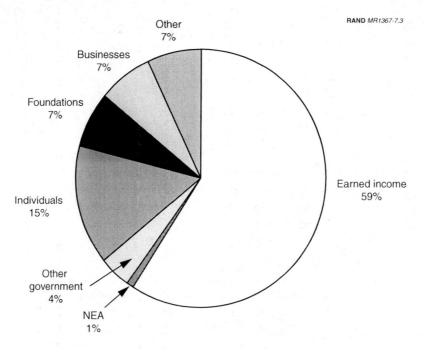

SOURCE: U.S. Census Bureau, 1997 Economic Census.

Figure 7.3—Sources of Revenue for Nonprofit Performing Arts
Organizations, 1997

KEY TRENDS

Direct Public Funding Declined Through Most of the 1990s

Direct government funding constitutes an important (although not the principal) source of revenue for nonprofit performing groups. However, as shown in Figure 7.4, after correcting for inflation, federal arts funding has been trending downward since the mid-1970s, while state and local funding climbed until the early 1990s. Since then, total government funding has been declining until recently. [11]

More striking than the downward trend in federal funding is the clear shift in direct funding from the federal to the state level, and increasingly to the local

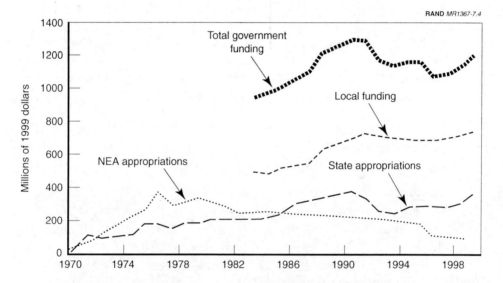

SOURCES: IRS Form 990, Business Master File Sample, National Endowment for the Arts, National Association of State Arts Agencies, Americans for the Arts.

NOTES: Local and state appropriations do not include NEA block grants. Components do not sum to total government funding because of differences in estimation methodologies.

Figure 7.4—Government Funding for the Arts, 1970–1999

[11]Until recently, data on government funding for the arts have not been reported in a comprehensive or systematic fashion. Thus, the data in Figure 7.4, which are based primarily on NEA reports, use different starting points.

level. Grants from these different levels of government differ in average size, the characteristics of their recipients, and the rationales for which they are given.[12] In particular, state and local governments tend to focus less on the arts per se and more on the social and economic benefits to local communities when awarding grants.

The subject of decentralization of government funding is known in the economics literature as "fiscal federalism," and has been popular for the last 20 years in the United States (Oates, 1999). There are several instruments for carrying out policy in this area, including taxes, debt instruments (e.g., bonds), and intergovernmental grants such as block grants, which are a major component of the NEA's annual budget.[13] The movement toward devolution of decisionmaking and financing to lower levels of government is motivated by the belief that local communities, which know local needs, can better use and administer funds for cultural programs than can the federal government. The sensitivity of state and local government funding for the arts to their constituencies is suggested by the fact that state arts agencies make approximately six times as many grants with less than twice as much money (DiMaggio, 1991). However, state and local arts council budgets are highly volatile and tend to vary both with the state of the economy and with the public's perception of the relative merits of various demands for taxpayer dollars (Brooks, 1997). To the extent that local arts organizations are reliant on local government funding, this situation may create substantial volatility in their budgets.

Indeed, comparisons of overall funding levels among the various levels of government do not provide a clear enough picture of the impact of state and local grants on local performing arts agencies because the populations these grants are designed to serve differ dramatically. Figure 7.5 demonstrates this point by comparing total funding and per capita funding for the arts from the NEA, the Georgia Council for the Arts, and the Atlanta Bureau of Cultural Affairs. Although the budget of the NEA is nearly 100 times that of the Atlanta Bureau of Cultural Affairs, the arts funding per capita is ten times higher for the latter than it is for the former. In other words, local government funding has greater fiscal impact on local communities than does federal funding.

---

[12]The most detailed treatment of this issue is contained in DiMaggio (1991). Although DiMaggio suggests that the difference in federal and state funding patterns and priorities is less pronounced than one might expect, his conclusions are based primarily on evidence from the 1980s.

[13]In fiscal 2000, for example, 40 percent of the NEA's $96.7 million budget was targeted for block grants.

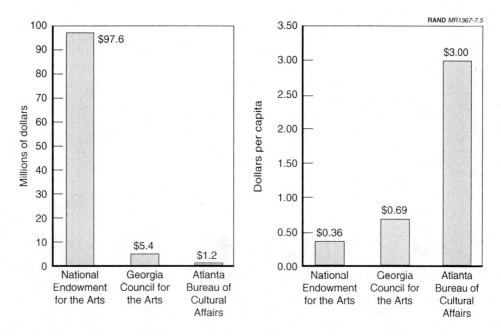

SOURCES: NEA, Georgia Council for the Arts, and Atlanta Bureau of Cultural Affairs, 2000.

Figure 7.5—Fiscal Year 2000 Budgets and Appropriations per Capita for Arts
Agencies at Three Levels of Government

Private Contributions Have Been Climbing, but Funding Practices Are Changing

Private contributions from individuals, business, and foundations together constitute the final source of unearned revenues for nonprofit arts organizations. As shown earlier in Figure 7.3, contributions from individuals are the largest of these sources—approximately twice the size of foundation grants and contributions from business. As demonstrated in Figure 7.6, the average contribution from each of these sources has generally been increasing, although not without some interruptions. For example, contributions from these sources were relatively flat from 1987 through 1992, no doubt reflecting the moderate recession during that period.

Contributions from individuals increased more than any other single source of philanthropic support, particularly between 1992 and 1997. Overall, however, common intuition among arts administrators is that these totals reflect greater

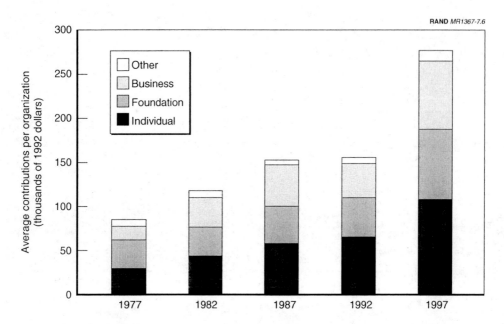

SOURCE: NEA (1998b, c, d); U.S. Bureau of the Census, 1997 Economic Census; and authors' calculations.

Figure 7.6—Philanthropic Giving to the Arts, 1977–1997

numbers of small donations rather than increased donation amounts from individual donors. Indeed, as generous individual patrons of the arts get older, the charitable sector has become increasingly concerned about who will replace them (Balfe, 1989). Arts organizations are also facing higher costs of fundraising as they pursue a greater number of individual donors.

Financial support from corporations has generally been increasing, but their funding practices appear to be changing. Corporate donors have moved away from unrestricted grants and are increasingly providing support in the form of targeted categorical support—limiting the flexibility of the arts organizations that receive it (Useem, 1990; Cobb, 1996). Similarly, although support to arts organizations from foundations has increased, foundations have also become increasingly focused on the effect of their grants on increasing access to the arts and on the broader benefits they provide (Renz and Lawrence, 1998).

In sum, although private philanthropy has played a critical role in sustaining the nonprofit performing arts over the past two decades, changes in funding patterns at the individual, foundation, and corporate levels have increased the costs of raising this money and placed new constraints on how nonprofit firms may use those funds.

Earned Income Has Been Stable and Costs Do Not Appear to Be Rising

Despite anecdotes about empty concert halls and unsold ballet tickets, aggregate trends in earned income for nonprofit performing groups display no clear long-term trend. As shown in Figure 7.7, earned income as a percentage of total revenues for the nonprofit performing arts followed no clear upward or downward trend. By and large, this is also true for each of the four arts disciplines.

Although this comparison suggests that the earnings gap facing the professional nonprofit performing arts sector has not been increasing, it also means that it has not been shrinking. Thus, nonprofit organizations appear to be about as dependent upon contributed income as they have been in the past. Moreover, this is true despite intensive efforts at marketing and audience development, and despite sharp rises in the cost of tickets. Average ticket prices for symphony orchestras, for example, increased 70 percent between 1985 and 1995.[14]

Unfortunately, Census data do not include information on numbers of performances or seats sold, so we cannot look at what has happened to per-unit costs

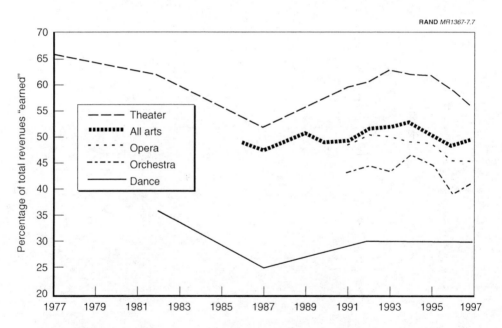

SOURCES: U.S. Bureau of the Census (1977–1997), IRS Form 990 data (1991–1997), Business Master File sample (1986–1990).

Figure 7.7—Earned Income as Percentage of Total Revenues, 1977–1997

[14]This figure is based on data from the American Symphony Orchestra League.

for the universe of live performing arts organizations during the 1990s. However, as shown in Figure 7.8, changes in the average real total expenditures of nonprofit performing companies (measured in 1992 dollars) varied considerably by discipline during the period 1987–1997.[15] Nonprofit classical music organizations, for example—mostly symphony orchestras—saw very large cost declines, averaging almost 3 percent per year over the ten-year period. Opera companies, on the other hand, saw their average costs rise by over 2 percent per year. On net, movements in costs across these disciplines tended to cancel each other out.

Nonprofit Performing Groups Remain Under Financial Pressure

Because the data presented in Figure 7.8 have not been adjusted to reflect output measures such as numbers of performances or attendees, positive or negative changes could simply represent changes in output per company rather

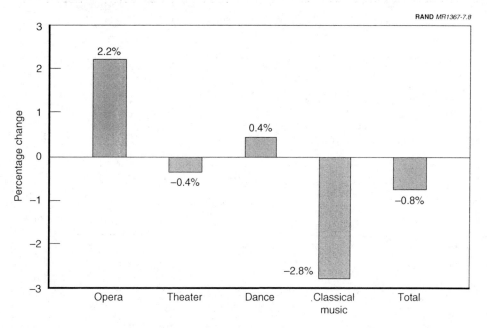

SOURCE: U.S. Census Bureau, 1998 Economic Census.

Figure 7.8—Annual Percentage Changes in Average Real Expenditures of Nonprofit Performing Arts Companies, 1987–1997

[15]Lack of data for the category "other music" precludes its inclusion here.

than changes in the cost of producing a fixed output, such as a performance. For example, the increase in average total expenditures of opera companies portrayed in Figure 7.8 could reflect an increase in the number of performances per opera company. Alternatively, average real expenses, like the changes in average real revenues reported in the previous chapter, could reflect the entrance or exit of small, low-cost companies into and out of the field.[16] Unfortunately, it is impossible to tell from existing data. In all likelihood, both of these factors—changes in output per company and changes in average company size—are operating.

An important question raised by these data is to what extent nonprofit performing companies can cut costs and still remain faithful to their artistic and other missions. A related question is whether rising costs should be seen as a sign of financial health or financial weakness. The key to both questions lies in the various strategies that performing companies have available to them in the face of incipient cost escalations, earned revenue declines, changes in the magnitude or focus of unearned revenues, or any combination of the three.

For-Profit Firms Also Face Increasing Financial Pressures

Up to now, our discussion in this chapter has focused on professional nonprofit live performing groups. It is important to note, however, that for-profit firms are also facing financial pressures. Although we lack systematic data on these firms, industry estimates suggest that for-profit firms involved in the production of the recorded arts have seen both the risks and the potential rewards from projects soar (Vogel, 1998). Although the payoff from blockbuster hits has become enormous, fewer projects in the commercial sector are earning enough to cover their production, marketing, and distribution costs. Nine out of ten commercial recording projects, for example, fail to break even. Two-thirds of commercial films are money losers, as are 70 percent of all theater productions (Vogel, 1998). In the face of rapidly evolving technologies and global competition, the shape of the commercial arts world is undergoing reconstruction as firms merge and enter into joint production agreements. In music, for example, as we mentioned in the previous chapter, the traditional six major recording labels have now been reduced to four, and some analysts have predicted further mergers are still to come in the next few years (Strauss, 2000).

---

[16]This interpretation, however, would seem to indicate that the nonprofit classical music industry had the greatest number of new entrants, which is inconsistent with the evidence presented in Chapter Six.

Organizations Are Using Multiple Strategies to Deal with Financial Pressures

There is a good deal of evidence to demonstrate that the business managers and artistic directors of performing arts organizations—both for-profit and nonprofit—pursue a number of strategies to deal with financial pressures. Although we have no systematic data, many case studies of individual organizations have documented these efforts, which include both cost-cutting and revenue-enhancing strategies. In addition, a few recent studies also point to the adoption of creative new financing strategies.

On the cost side, strategies include:

1.   Reducing real wage growth

2.   Choosing productions or pieces that require fewer artists and/or fewer scene changes

3.   Hiring fewer expensive guest artists

4.   Avoiding newer works to avoid royalty payments to creators

5.   Cutting rehearsal times

6.   Developing productions in low-cost locations.

On the revenue side, strategies include:

7.   Producing lavish programs featuring celebrity artists to attract large audiences (blockbusters)

8.   Producing familiar, traditional programs ("warhorses") designed to attract large audiences (the "Nutcracker" strategy)

9.   Tying primary programming to sales of auxiliary products such as T-shirts, collectibles, etc.

10.   Increasing the number of performances of the same production

11.   Maximizing the audience per performance by increasing the size of performance venues

12.   Targeting niche markets that have predictable, loyal audiences.

On the financing side, strategies include:

13.   Productions jointly financed by firms in the for-profit and nonprofit sectors

14.   Adoption by nonprofits of commercial financing techniques such as for-profit subsidiaries or charitable component mutual funds.[17]

In the next section, we describe several of these strategies and the kinds of organizations that are most able to take advantage of them. As we point out, the size of an organization's budget often determines which strategies will be most effective. Midsized organizations, for example, tend to find it more difficult to reduce labor costs than large organizations do, for reasons we describe below.

In making size distinctions, however, we cannot be too precise. We cannot define small, midsized, and large organizations based on arbitrary dividing lines between the sizes of their budgets, because such lines would differ over time, across disciplines and sectors, and across function within the performing arts delivery system and across locations.[18] Therefore, as a rough guide, for this analysis we define a midsized live performing organization as one that relies on predominantly professional—that is, paid—artistic personnel and has a formal, paid administrative staff (probably including an artistic director and/or business manager, a development director, and various clerical workers), but is not in the very top ranks of its field. For example, with respect to the orchestra classifications used by the American Symphony Orchestra League (ASOL), our category "midsized" would include most "regional," "metropolitan," and "urban" orchestras (with 1991 budgets of between approximately $650,000 and $8.5 million), whereas our category "small" would be the volunteer-sector orchestras that the ASOL calls "community" orchestras, and "large" would comprise "major" orchestras. A small recorded arts organization would be a firm that has roughly 1 to 50 paid employees; a large firm would have over 500 paid employees.

Wage-Based Cost Control Strategies (Strategy 1) Disadvantage Midsized Performing Organizations. Baumol and Baumol (1985a) suggest that one common strategy for controlling cost growth in nonprofit performing companies is to cut the real salaries of both artists and managers by allowing nominal salary increases to fall below the rate of inflation. In fact, during periods of high inflation, there is evidence that this approach has been widespread across both nonprofit and for-profit organizations in service industries such as health and education. It has been less often used, presumably because it is less effective, when prices have been relatively stable.[19]

---

[17]These are mutual funds that would link personal investment with contributing to the arts. For examples of these and other financing techniques being explored by nonprofits, see Williams (1998).

[18]Given differences in the cost of living, a $2 million budget in New York City might be regarded as small, but the same budget in Fargo, North Dakota, would be considered large.

[19]See, for example, Baumol (1996).

In the performing arts, union contracts preclude many, if not most, large and midsized performing companies from either reducing nominal wages or downsizing union labor, so that financial pressures tend to fall most heavily on non-union personnel (at least initially). When this happens, large performing companies have an advantage over midsized ones, because they tend to have a larger volunteer base from which they can draw for administrative, and sometimes also artistic, labor (Blau et al., 1986). Because large organizations tend to have lengthier series of identical programs per season, they are also better able to economize on artistic personnel costs by holding fewer expensive rehearsals (Schwarz, 1983)—although this strategy may work better in some disciplines than others. Small volunteer sector organizations, since they tend to rely heavily on volunteers in the first place, are less likely to suffer escalating personnel costs.

Reducing Production Size and Eliminating Guest Stars (Strategy 2) Is Likely To Shrink Audiences. Baumol and Baumol (1985a) provide some insight into the "shrinking the size of productions" strategy, showing that between 1946 and approximately 1976, Broadway theater companies reduced the average cast size for nonmusical productions from 16 to 8. Unfortunately, we have no hard data to show whether this trend has continued, but we do have some supportive anecdotal evidence.[20] Dunn (1984), for example, describes how, during the recession of the early 1980s, some Broadway producers limited the size of both casts and crews and chose only to produce shows with minimal sets. Dunn also describes the concessions made by the theatrical unions during this time, which included reductions in staffing as well as reductions in wage rates. More recently, Phillips (2001) argues that the very definition of a "large-cast" play in the nonprofit theater has shrunk from approximately 30 to 35 actors in the 1960s and 1970s to somewhere between 8 and 12 actors in the late 1990s.

The production-shrinking strategy is probably most common among mid-budget performing groups. Ironically, according to Phillips, most large-cast plays are produced at low-cost, non-union theaters and performance spaces that seat fewer than 100. The big-budget companies also put on big productions, with elaborate sets and large celebrity casts, in the expectation that large audiences will allow revenues to outstrip costs. But although mid-budget companies, like big-budget groups, must cope with union payscales and significant administrative overhead costs, unlike their larger cousins they could risk bankruptcy with the commercial failure of a single big production.

---

[20] For example, although the Theatre Communications Group publishes annual "season preview" listings of its members' productions, no cast size information is provided. See Heilbrun (2001b) for reprint of data misprinted in original Baumol and Baumol (1985a) article.

Unfortunately, as we discussed in Chapter Four, minimalist approaches toward productions may end up shrinking audiences by more than they shrink costs.

Only Big Budget Organizations Can Afford High-Cost Productions and Celebrity Artists (Strategy 7). In order to attract large audiences, organizations must spend heavily on advertising and promotion. They have found that the presence of "bankable" stars greatly improves their chances of success by bringing with them preestablished audiences. In fact, our anecdotal evidence suggests that both live and recorded arts organizations—if they have the budgets for it—are now choosing programming strategies featuring blockbuster productions and star-studded casts (Pogrebin, 2000a and 2000b).

Of course, the origins of this strategy are not new: Prima donnas such as Jenny Lind and Adelina Patti were heavily and successfully promoted to American audiences in the mid-19th century. But marketing campaigns and superstars are expensive and getting more so, causing the breakeven point for profitability to rise. As a result, many for-profit firms have decided that bigger is better, and merger and acquisition activity in the entertainment industry has exploded in the mid- to late-1990s. Many nonprofit performing organizations are also beginning to face a situation in which they must either maximize the size of their audience or refocus their programming in order to survive.[21]

Although not yet evident in Economic Census data, one reason may be that uncertain funding streams, as described in a previous section of this chapter, are forcing nonprofit organizations to rely more than ever on earned income. Another reason is that contributors, and particularly foundation and corporate contributors, are increasingly looking for evidence of audience penetration as a condition for receiving the funding they do provide (Useem 1990; Renz and Lawrence, 1998). But this increased reliance on the market bears a cost: more money spent on marketing, splashy shows, and star-studded programs. This strategy in turn requires even bigger audiences to support the resulting cost increases, and so on—creating an upward spiral of audience and budget growth. Like the for-profit firms, in such an environment only the biggest firms can survive.

Increasing Reliance on Warhorse Programming (Strategy 8) Is a Widespread Revenue-Building Strategy. One of the most frequently expressed charges against performing companies, and especially mid-budget organizations, is that increasingly they are relying on "warhorse" programming—that is, traditional works beloved by general audiences—to increase their box office and please

---

[21]Audience or client size maximization is frequently posited to be a major objective of nonprofit firms. See, for example, Newhouse (1970) and Hansmann (1981). Lange et al. (1986) provide limited empirical evidence for this trend.

contributors. From the perspective of those who place a high value on artistic innovation this complaint is understandable, but the practice has been around for a long time. A major reason is that, as we discussed in Chapter Four, a majority of the people who attend live performances are "casual attendees" who are much more likely to be attracted to traditional works than to more innovative fare. The question is whether underlying changes in the funding environment, as well as in the sociodemographics of audiences, have caused companies to rely more on warhorses than they used to.

In one of the few studies bearing on this issue, Pierce (2000) uses data on 64 members of OPERA America to explore the impact of variations in local culture and sources of contributed income on programmatic risk-taking and experimentation in opera. Using the frequency of an opera's performance between 1989 and 1994 as a measure of its risk, he finds that the relative wealth and educational level of the local population is positively correlated with risk-taking. For instance, the wealthier and better educated the local community, the more likely an opera company is to perform Wagner's *Siegfried* rather than Puccini's *La Boheme*. Even more interesting, Pierce finds that federal government support (from the NEA) is positively correlated with programmatic innovation, while local government support is even more strongly positively correlated with programmatic conservatism.

Pierce's findings are consistent with the view that Americans' interest in innovative programming should increase as they become wealthier and better educated. However, his work also suggests that recent increases in state and local support for the arts, relative to federal support, may adversely impact artistic innovation. Which effect is dominant? Research by Heilbrun (2001a) throws some additional light on the matter. Heilbrun analyzes programming data from the growing OPERA America membership for selected years between the 1982–1983 and 1997–1998 seasons. Based on measures of the diversity of the aggregate opera repertory in each year (number of productions times number of companies), Heilbrun finds evidence of a distinct decline in the diversity of American—but not Canadian—opera company repertory beginning in the 1991–1992 season, and specifically a significant decline in the number of 20th century operas produced. Although several explanations are possible—and the time period considered is rather short—Heilbrun's results are consistent with the view that American opera companies have been shifting their programming toward a more popular, less demanding repertory in response to changing funding patterns. In Canada, where public support for opera is far more generous, no such shift has occurred.[22]

---

[22]Rising production costs and the high cost of commercial failures may incline private investors and perhaps even private donors to favor warhorse programs as well.

Replication Strategies of Performing Groups Have Had Mixed Success (Strategy 10). Increasing the number of performances of the same production can be seen as either a cost-cutting or revenue-enhancing strategy. If effective, it spreads the fixed costs of production over a larger revenue base. However, if fixed costs rise significantly as a result of the replication, the resulting cost growth can swamp any positive increments to revenue.

A traditional way to pursue this strategy is to take the show on the road because touring enables companies to dip into their established repertoire without having to develop new material. Indeed, touring has been a mainstay of all types of performing arts companies since colonial times (Butsch, 2000). However, it by no means provides an automatic boost to net income.[23] For example, although 75 percent of respondents to a 1990 survey conducted by Chamber Music America reported some touring activity, just 55 percent claimed it had been profitable for them. Another 12 percent reported that they had actually lost money on the tour. According to the authors of the report, the biggest and best-known ensembles were more likely to have profitable tours because they were better able to market themselves to presenters and audiences (Chamber Music America, 1992).

In a variation on this theme, Cowan (1987, p.24) refers to the growing popularity of the "second home" concept, whereby instead of or in addition to touring, a performing organization "produces a regular recurring schedule of performances in a location other than its home base and seeks an ongoing relationship with that community." However, cities that are potential "second homes" generally prefer to host established companies with strong artistic reputations. And of course, the strategy doesn't always work: One of the most famous companies to adopt this strategy, the Joffrey Ballet, experienced severe financial problems in the early 1990s despite (or perhaps because of) part-time homes it had established in New York and Los Angeles (Smith, 1995).

Broadway theaters have long relied on the economies of scale of a successful run to lower costs and achieve profitability, but the average size of the Broadway audience used to be smaller. Moreover, as shown in Figure 7.9, the distribution of runs on Broadway has changed. During the 1920s slightly more than 10 percent of productions folded immediately (after less than 10 performances); well over 75 percent fell into the middle range between 10 and 300 performances. Less than 5 percent were "smash hits" (plays that ran for more than 300 performances), and none ran for more than 450 performances. By the 1960s, however, there had been a substantial rise in the number of productions

---

[23]In fact, in many cases touring may not be perceived as a cost-reducing (or for that matter, revenue-enhancing) strategy, at least in the short-term. Many performing groups consider touring a matter of prestige—and of mission.

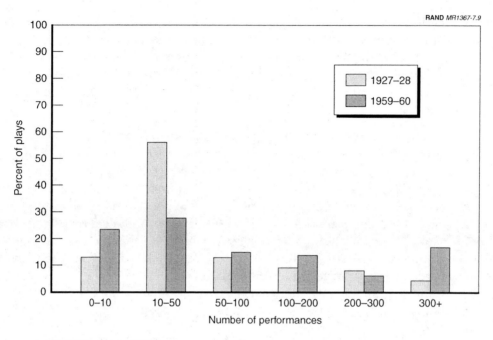

RAND *MR1367-7.9*

SOURCE: Moore (1968).

**Figure 7.9—Distribution of Performances for Broadway Plays, 1927–28
and 1959–60 Seasons**

that attracted large audiences. Almost 25 percent of productions folded before
they achieved 10 performances, but almost 20 percent ran for more than 300
performances.

By the mid-1990s, the growing fixed costs of advertising had further exacer-
bated Broadway's tendency to divide between smash hits and outright flops.[24]
Vogel (1998) estimates that, as of approximately 1995, a play with running costs
of $100,000 per week, average ticket prices of $30, and seating of 500 required
an average capacity utilization of almost 85 percent (417 paying audience
members per performance) just to break even. This compares to a break-even
capacity of 55 percent estimated by Moore (1968) for the early 1960s. But despite the fact that the odds against seeing a positive return on investment are
now well over 2 to 1, individual investors and large entertainment companies
continue to be attracted to Broadway. This is because, when shows are successful, they are very successful: According to Vogel (1998, pp. 382–383), as of

---

[24]The cost of putting on a Broadway production rose by approximately 100 percent between the
early 1980s and the mid-1990s (Vogel, 1998).

February 1989 the hit musical *Cats*, for example, had earned more than 11 times its initial investment from its North American box office alone.

This boom-or-bust pattern is more evident in the recorded segment of the performing arts industry, for which increasing replication of the same product is always a goal. For example, according to Denisoff (1975), in 1968 the average popular music album had to sell approximately 7,800 copies to break even. By the early 1980s, the number had risen to 100,000 copies (Garvin, 1981). Vogel (1998) estimates that, as of the 1990s, perhaps no more than 10 percent of all new releases made money. But these 10 percent were generally profitable enough to offset the losses on the other 90 percent. Similarly, the high fixed operating costs for radio and especially television networks meant that the gain or loss of a few prime-time rating points could trigger either immense profits or immense losses.

The strategy with perhaps the greatest potential for reducing per-unit costs and increasing revenues for midsized and larger live performing arts firms is to increase the size of the performance venue. For many performing organizations this has apparently been achieved to great effect through electronic amplification, which is allowing both small groups and single artists to play to much larger halls. Again, although systematic data are missing, anecdotal evidence abounds that audio technologies such as body microphones have become common not only at large theaters (roughly 500 seats and up) but also at midsized theaters (200 to 500 seats).[25] Even some opera houses and concert halls are apparently beginning to succumb to the lure of electronically enhanced acoustics, which, according to some observers, American performing arts audiences are beginning both to expect and demand (Tommasini, 2000a).

Of course, the ultimate increase in size of "venue" involves either replicating productions through recorded media or broadcasting them live over radio or television. Here music clearly has a great advantage over other art forms such as theater or dance. From the 1940s through to the 1980s, many of the most influential advances in music recording technology—such as long playing records, hi-fidelity sound, magnetic tape, and digital recording—were developed in an effort to capture the audio-dynamics of, and thus the audience for, live orchestral music (Frith, 1986). But, at least in recent years, actual income from broadcasting and recording has been a relatively small contributor to the total revenues of most symphony orchestras. Data on 173 members of ASOL reveal that broadcasting and recording as a percentage of total income hovered around 2.2

---

[25]See, for example, Phillips (2001).

percent between 1988 and 1990.[26] For opera companies, per-company average revenue from broadcasting fell from 2.4 percent of total income during the decade of the 1980s to just 0.1 percent of total income from 1990 to 1998 (OPERA America, various years).

The outlook for the future is grim. According to von Rhein (2000), where once the market for recorded classical music contained six multinational recording giants, now there are only three, each of which is drastically cutting back its classical music divisions. The reason is their unprofitability: BMG Classics, for example, a subdivision of the giant Bertelsmann media conglomerate, reportedly lost $6 million in 1999. In response to the cutbacks, some orchestras have tried to create their own labels, but they have generally not been successful in attracting consumers. In the case of opera, recordings of selected scenes and arias sung by individual opera stars have done quite well on the classical music charts, but opera companies have been forced to seek corporate sponsorship to pay for recordings of entire operas (Johnson, 2000; Tommasini, 2000b).

Large Nonprofits Are Increasingly Adopting For-Profit Business Models To Stabilize Revenues (Strategies 9 and 13). As their productions grow larger and splashier and as the celebrity artists that ornament these productions grow increasingly more expensive, many large nonprofits are exploring some of the same revenue-enhancing and financing techniques that have long been popular among for-profit firms from Hollywood producers to sports shoe manufacturers. Merchandising, for example, has become big business. T-shirts and coffee mugs display not only the title of the latest show, but, for marquee companies like the New York City Ballet, the name of the company itself. Like Reebok or Nike, New York City Ballet's name has become an exploitable brand name, soon to be stamped on little girls' leotards, shirts, and shorts sold across the country (*Dance Magazine*, 2001).

Large nonprofits are also becoming more creative with their financing. In theater, for example, many nonprofit regional and off-Broadway theaters now accept "enhancement money" in return for acting as testing grounds for potential future commercial runs.[27] According to the President's Committee on the Arts and Humanities (1997), 44 percent of the new plays produced on Broadway between 1975 and 1995 originated in the nonprofit sector. Perhaps the most prominent recent partnership between nonprofit theater and the for-profit world—although not, in this case, Broadway—is the one between New York's Roundabout Theater Company and American Airlines. American's $8.5 million

---

[26]We recognize that these figures are averages across all symphonies and the returns to some especially prominent orchestras may be somewhat higher because of their reputations.

[27]Note that not every arrangement of this sort involves enhancement money.

payment helped to underwrite a $25 million refurbishment of Roundabout's new 750-seat American Airlines Theater on West 42nd Street (Pogrebin, 2000a and 2000b). According to at least some observers, resident theaters' pursuit of Broadway-style success has resulted in minimal distinctions between nonprofit and for-profit programming, with both sides of the 501(c)(3) aisle now pursuing the safe and familiar, rather than the artistically innovative and financially risky (Landesman, 2000; Brustein, 2000). Others, however, believe this trend to be less applicable to small nonprofits, which are more innovative in their programming.

For Small Commercial and Nonprofit Organizations, Niche Markets Are an Answer, but Not for Midsized Groups (Strategy 12). Anecdotal evidence also suggests that the goal of large-scale replication of star-studded programs and products is moving beyond the reach of all but the largest organizations. For many small for-profit and especially volunteer organizations, this is not a concern: Their programming strategies focus on niche rather than general audiences. In the for-profit recorded music sector, for example, small independent record producers and labels representing distinct musical styles commonly act as intermediaries between artists and the major record companies (Vogel, 1998). Although most are still dependent on the major labels for their initial financing and for the manufacturing of CDs, the advent of Internet technologies may allow some of these firms (and many more individual artists) to circumvent the majors by creating their own web-based rather than CD-based distribution systems. The Internet already is allowing them to market themselves and their artists directly to potential consumers scattered across the country—and across the world (Vogel, 1998; Gomes, 2000).

Most volunteer-sector performing companies are even less able and generally less interested than for-profits in competing for the superstars or creating the blockbusters that would put them in front of mass audiences. By definition, their performances and productions draw heavily on the large pool of low-paid or volunteer nonprofessional artists that live and work in their local communities.[28] They may or may not be incorporated as formal 501(c)(3) corporations under the U.S. Tax Code. By far the majority do not have their own permanent performance spaces, and they tend to be heavily reliant on the artistic vision and management skills of individual founders (Jeffri, 1980; Bowles, 1992).

This is not to say, however, that volunteer-sector performing groups as a whole do not want to grow, or that they do not want to reach beyond their current niches to attract bigger audiences. But many are committed to experimental art

---

[28]As discussed in Chapter Five, the term "nonprofessional" simply describes artists whose primary incomes do not come from the arts. It does not necessarily denote lack of professional training or artistic ability.

forms or art forms that draw on a non-European ethnic or cultural heritage, and are strongly opposed to "mainstreaming" their programs in ways that might be required to attract larger and more diversified audiences (Yoshitomi, 1991). Still others have tried to grow, or even have achieved some growth, only to be forced to downsize again in response to the vagaries of funders and the market.

The field of modern dance provides a good example of the obstacles to growth facing small performing groups that lack a potential audience that is easily reached and economically significant.[29] As described by Jeffri (1980), and we believe it is still true today, most modern dance groups do not have the capital to purchase or lease their own permanent performance spaces. Lack of a permanent home limits their potential for earnings growth in at least two ways: It makes them heavily reliant on touring, which typically involves fixed contractual fees for performances rather than box office ticket sales, and it restricts their ability to capitalize on a successful run because engagements are limited. Further, because modern dance companies are constantly on tour, they can find it difficult to build local constituencies for their work. This in turn makes it difficult to raise the capital necessary to establish a permanent performing space. A vicious cycle is created.

However, as Jeffri and others have emphasized, an even worse situation may be created when public and private funders "artificially" inflate small companies' budgets with large capital infusions. For example, according to Jeffri (1980, p. 62), one of the implicit (or sometimes explicit) conditions for accepting government funding is expansion of a company's scale of operations, whether it is ready, willing, or able to do so, and whether there is demand for its increased output in the long term. Quoting from Siegel (1977) with respect to dance, Jeffri reports:

> Dance is on a six-lane escalator with a two-lane road at the top. Since the advent of government subsidy . . . all dance companies have been under pressure to expand their operations—to do more performances so they can reach more audience, which will produce bigger budgets and more employment for dancers.

Bowles (1992, p. 61) reports a similar phenomenon in the context of small, ethnically specific arts organizations, which are "reaching maturity at a time when funding from all sources has leveled off or is undergoing severe cutbacks." Responses to a 1990 survey of more than 1700 such ethnically specific organizations (including visual and multidisciplinary arts organizations) indicated that many were being forced to cut back on personnel as well as programs during

---

[29]The modifier "economically significant" is important here because lack of financial support does not necessarily imply lack of interest. This is especially relevant to organizations based in economically disadvantaged communities.

the period because their earned and contributed income growth failed to catch up to cost growth.

In sum, focusing on niche markets can work well for small organizations whose costs are also relatively low. With the advent of the Internet, recorded arts organizations in particular may be able to expand their niche audiences beyond the traditional limitations of geography and time. For live performing organizations in the mid-budget range, however, the relatively high fixed costs associated with administration and real estate mean they are quite vulnerable to even short-term shifts in earned or contributed income. To stabilize the earned income and perhaps also the contributed income components of their budgets, such organizations must either downsize in order to concentrate on niche markets, or position themselves to become acknowledged regional, national, or even global leaders, with the attendant increases in revenues and costs.[30]

FUTURE ISSUES

Despite data constraints that limit our analysis,[31] the financial picture we have drawn suggests that the earnings gap described by Baumol and Bowen over 30 years ago remains a key feature of the nonprofit professional performing arts world today. Indeed, judging by the stagnant levels of earned income as a percentage of revenues—despite improved marketing and higher ticket prices—the average nonprofit performing arts organization remains highly vulnerable to the whims of contributors—and increasingly, to the whims of the market.

Government Support

Looking to the future, we see several issues that bear watching with respect to the finances and strategies of performing arts organizations. First, government support for the arts increasingly means state and municipal government support. Although this shift may mean that government funding is more responsive to the needs of local arts organizations, it may also mean increased volatility in funding and a more conservative approach to the art that is funded. An increase in artistic conservatism will affect all nonprofit professional performing organi-

---

[30]Melanie Beene and Associates (1988) perceptively analyze the case of a mid-budget performing organization that failed to negotiate these two extremes: the Oakland Symphony. According to the authors, a probable contributor to that orchestra's eventual bankruptcy was its failure to establish itself as a distinct alternative to the much larger San Francisco Symphony across the bay—even as it tried to join the ranks of the nation's major orchestras. Faced with an inflexible musicians' union, stable or shrinking audiences, and large operating deficits from its attempt to create a multipurpose performing arts center, the Oakland Symphony simply collapsed under its own weight.

[31]These data constraints have limited the picture we are able to paint in two ways. First, they restrict our ability to compare costs with revenues. Second, they limit our focus to the nonprofit sector.

zations, whereas increased volatility will disproportionately affect midsized organizations that have relatively high fixed costs and relatively poor potential for audience expansion. The shift is also likely to mean less emphasis on the arts per se and more on their social and economic benefits to local communities. Whether this is good or bad depends on one's views about the primary goals and purposes of art.

Private Philanthropy

Second, private philanthropy has seen large increases over the past few decades. But, as with state and local funding, this expansion has implications for programming. As artists and organizations increasingly rely on grantmakers such as corporate foundations for support, the art that reaches audiences may increasingly reflect the tastes and values of local communities and specific benefactors. Once again, whether this is good or bad depends on one's views about the goals and purposes of art.

Private philanthropy does not exist in a vacuum: There is a substantial literature that suggests that government support for the arts may displace or crowd out private grants and donations to a greater or lesser extent (Steinberg, 1993). Although the relationship between private and public funding is complex,[32] some studies suggest that each dollar of public funding may crowd out between 10 and 50 cents in private support (Brooks, 2000b, 2000c; Kingma, 1989). If these findings are correct, then private giving to nonprofit arts organizations in the future may well be stimulated if government support continues to fall in real terms but on less than a one-to-one basis. If government funding increases, however, private giving may decrease but total funding would go up.

Diversification of Income Sources

What seems clear from this discussion is that nonprofit institutions are likely to be best served by diversifying their sources of contributed income, thus minimizing the effects of any one source on both the volatility of their budgets and the freedom of their programming. How successful different types of nonprofits will be in this endeavor may well depend upon their ability to be perceived as adding value to their communities. Many large, well-established, prestigious organizations have already created this perception. For smaller organizations that rely more on volunteer and in-kind contributions and may already be serving well-defined, if more limited audiences, cultivating this perception may

---

[32]Many government funding advocates, for example, believe that government funding is an effective tool for leveraging private support (American Assembly, 1997).

be less important. For organizations in between, the prospects are less clear. They may well be forced to reconsider what audiences they are trying to reach and how.

Emphasis on Earned Income

Potentially even more significant, although difficult to isolate in the available data, is a fourth issue: nonprofit professional performing groups' increasing emphasis on tickets sold and merchandise purchased in addition to the nature and quality of the art they produce. As described above, most of the revenue-enhancing strategies large and midsized groups are pursuing are designed to increase earned, rather than contributed, income (although this may be a false dichotomy because many institutional benefactors now require measurable audience-building efforts as a precondition for giving). In any case, as these nonprofit organizations rely more and more on the market to pay their bills, it is almost inevitable that they will look more like for-profit organizations. This could raise serious issues about the appropriate distinctions between tax-exempt nonprofits and taxable for-profits. It also has implications for the type of art that will be produced.

For small professional nonprofits, audience focus will also be the rule, but not necessarily in the bigger-is-better context. The departure of larger organizations for bigger pastures could give these groups an opportunity to build and retain a comparatively small but loyal set of followers who would value their unique artistic contributions and be willing to pay for them as both consumers and patrons of the arts. Technological developments such as the Internet may help these groups to establish and expand their niches. Without major efforts at arts education, however, they will be unable to attract mass audiences unless they significantly alter their existing programming.

Finally, the prospects for midsized nonprofit institutions are not rosy. The declines and reorientations in public and private sector funding are likely to push many of them toward traditional programming and fairly mainstream artistic endeavors in order to build audiences and grow organizationally. However, because most lack the resources to put on blockbusters, and because of the downward trend in transportation and communication costs, it is not clear how well they can compete with respect to world-famous and celebrity-heavy institutions located in major metropolitan areas. Further, like all groups dedicated to live performances, these institutions must also compete with recorded blockbusters of the past, which are steadily improving in quality and availability.

Chapter Eight

WHERE ARE THE PERFORMING ARTS HEADED?

In the previous chapters we have described the current shape of the performing arts environment and identified major trends that bear watching in each of the four domains of the performing arts world: audiences, artists, organizations, and financing. In this final chapter, we first present a picture of America's future performing arts environment and then discuss what this might mean for the quantity, quality, and availability of the performing arts. Next, we discuss how arts policy might be refocused in light of those developments. Finally, we suggest what future research would help answer many of the unresolved issues we have identified.

A VISION OF THE FUTURE

The art world we envision for the future remains highly segmented, but the divisions are not the same as those that existed during most of the 20th century. Instead of a sharp demarcation between a nonprofit sector producing high art and a for-profit sector producing mass entertainment, the major divisions in the future will be along the lines of big versus small arts organizations, and firms that target broad versus niche markets.

Specifically, if current trends continue, we envision an arts environment that is increasingly segmented into distinct sectors, each specializing in a particular type of product or artistic experience, targeting a different market, and responding to specific financial pressures. We describe these sectors below:

- **A large commercial sector characterized by fewer but increasingly larger firms catering to popular mass markets, often on a global scale.** Faced with an environment in which the rewards of success and the costs of failure can be enormous (and the latter outnumber the former by a significant margin), this sector will seek to minimize its risks by choosing conservative programming that relies on established stars and formats and is designed to appeal to the broadest possible audiences. It will continue to serve as the principal purveyor of popular entertainment for the mass market—a market that will continue to grow in response to population and income growth.

- **A small commercial sector characterized by small firms that target niche markets within the recorded branches of the performing arts.** Often these firms will move into areas, such as classical recordings, that the large commercial firms have abandoned because they simply don't provide the margins and volume that larger for-profit firms require. The low costs of entry into this sector, combined with technological changes (such as the Internet and e-commerce) that relax the traditional constraints of geographically based market thresholds, will also enable these firms to serve a wider variety of smaller and more specialized markets. Indeed, lower entry costs and the ability to serve spatially dispersed specialized markets will provide firms within this sector the opportunity to be more adventuresome in the variety of programming they offer. Whether they will choose to do so may well depend upon their ability to identify and market to newly emerging specialized submarkets for the performing arts.

- **A small number of large nonprofits providing high-quality live performing arts in major metropolitan centers.** Like their large commercial-sector counterparts (and for many of the same reasons), these organizations too will seek to maximize their earned revenues from ticket sales and related business income. They will rely on advertising and marketing campaigns promoting celebrity performers and traditional materials designed to attract the broadest share of what appears to be a relatively stable market—those individuals who can pay premium prices to attend the highest-quality live performances.

- **A much larger number of small nonprofit performing arts organizations catering to local and specialized markets, particularly ethno-cultural and specialized markets.** Although earnings constitute a small fraction of these organizations' revenues, their low costs and access to contributed income and volunteer labor enable them to survive and, in some cases, prosper. For many small and midsized communities, these organizations will provide the major source of live professional performing arts—even if they do not feature the stars and grand productions that typify the large nonprofit sector.

- **An even larger and growing number of amateur performing arts organizations.** These organizations fill what appears to be a growing segment of the performing arts market—the demand for hands-on participation for avocational artists. As is true of small nonprofit organizations, earnings are not an important source of revenue for these institutions. Instead, they rely very heavily on local volunteers, not only for contributed income but also for performing and administrative labor. Because these organizations are primarily grass-roots organizations that are closely tied to their local communities, they may also be supported by local governments. Their numbers will be closely tied to the future size of the market for hands-on participation. Again, like their small nonprofit counterparts, these organizations will have little in common with the larger nonprofits in terms of programming, audience demographics, or the professional status of their artists.

- **A sizeable number of nonprofit presenting organizations that provide access to the live performing arts to residents outside major metropolitan areas.** As we noted in Chapter Six, we do not know enough about these organizations because they are typically embedded within non-arts organizations. But they are likely to become an increasingly important source of high-quality performing arts if, as we predict, the top-echelon live arts become concentrated in major metropolitan areas. University-based presenting organizations are likely to be especially important to the future of the performing arts because they serve multiple functions within the performing arts world. Not only are they major presenters, but they also play significant roles in training new artists and fostering innovation in the creation of new work.

The biggest challenge we foresee relates to the middle tier of nonprofit arts organizations, particularly those opera companies, symphony orchestras, ballet companies, and theater groups that service small and medium-sized cities across the country. The realities of aging audiences, escalating costs, and static or even declining funding streams will force these organizations into a serious rethinking of their primary mission, the audiences they want to reach, and their organizational structure. Some will choose to pursue increased local funding to keep up professional standards, go for the smash hit and superstar marquee, and aspire to become regional or national brand-name institutions. Others may opt to fill specialized niches based on particular kinds of programming that target specialized markets. Still others will decide to focus on their immediate community, using local talent to keep costs down and targeting programming to encourage participation by local audiences. Finally, some will simply wither away, unable to reconcile conflicts among their various stakeholders.

We currently have too little information on a number of issues to accurately gauge how closely this profile will accord with the actual future. The shape of change within the commercial sectors, for example, may well hinge on how critical intellectual property and e-commerce issues are resolved. Moreover, although middle-tier nonprofits face special challenges, they are often viewed by their communities as important civic assets. Thus, they may be able to generate sufficient public and private funding to sustain their operations. Finally, our projection of future demand assumes that observable trends will continue.

Given historical patterns of demand, this assumption appears to be reasonable. However, as we note below, policy interventions could increase future demand for the arts.

It is important to remember that we have been describing the performing arts system in very broad strokes and with highly aggregated data. Although such an approach may bring out connections among different parts of the arts world that are not captured in more focused studies, it cannot account for the diversity and particularity of the experience of different artistic subcultures. Even if some of our predictions about demand and organizational demographics turn out to be valid for the performing arts as a whole, the arts in different parts of the country and in different disciplines and subdisciplines may evolve in their own distinct way.

IMPLICATIONS FOR THE PERFORMING ARTS

We return to the question posed at the beginning of this report: Is the future we describe likely to be the best of times or the worst of times for the performing arts? Specifically, what are the likely effects on the quantity, quality, and availability of the arts if performing arts organizations continue to specialize as we predict?

As far as the quantity of artistic productions is concerned, the future looks bright. New and improved production, recording, and distribution technologies will allow American audiences to continue to enjoy a wide variety of performing arts, both whenever and wherever they like. Most arts programming will still be targeted at mass audiences, but some observers argue that the widespread popularity of mass entertainment—not only in the United States, but around the world—attests to its worth.

The number of professional-level live performances of the high arts, on the other hand, is likely to decline. It is not clear, however, whether this trend poses a threat to the public interest. If more people wanted to attend professional live performances in any community, the performers and presenters would not face financial problems there. This will surely be the case in major metropolitan areas where large institutions will continue to offer productions that feature the best that money and talent can offer. In addition, touring artists and performing arts companies will provide an opportunity for fans to attend live performances in the many smaller cities and towns that would otherwise not be able to sustain top-level performing arts. And for those who are not able to attend the live performance, high-quality digital recordings will provide an improved, if still imperfect, substitute for the live experience.

For Americans with less traditional artistic tastes, the future promises greater opportunities than ever before. The number of live performances in local communities is likely to grow. These will be mainly low-budget productions of great cultural and artistic diversity performed by artists on a volunteer basis. The number and range of non-live artistic productions should also increase as cable television, satellite broadcasting, and the Internet knock down geographic barriers to audience development. The ability to reach far-flung audiences has created healthy markets for forms of art that had previously been unable to attract economically significant demand. Although the commercial success of such ventures remains to be proven, it seems likely that in the future, niche arts markets will be not only possible but profitable. And for those who want to be directly involved in the creation of music, opera, theater, or dance, the proliferation of community-based groups will offer more and greater opportunities for direct participation in the performing arts at the amateur level.

How the quality of the arts will be affected by changes in the performing arts system is more difficult to analyze, primarily because quality is a subjective criterion. Still, it is an unavoidable issue when evaluating the continued vitality of the arts in America. The question of quality can be posed in at least two ways: First, will artists find sufficient opportunities to develop their skills within the future performing arts system? And second, will that system encourage the creation of original works of enduring value?

The polarization of artists' incomes (created by the superstar phenomenon), the greater concentration of large nonprofits, and a possible contraction in the number of midsized organizations are all trends that could reduce the opportunities for talented young people to pursue professional careers in the performing arts. In particular, many observers view midsized arts organizations as a vital training ground for actors, ballet dancers, opera singers, and classical musicians, preparing them for the leap to the "big leagues." If this middle tier contracts, many aspiring young talents could be forced to take jobs in the small nonprofit and volunteer sectors, where standards of production are far less professional.

These concerns, however, may be overblown. When a similar contraction of the middle tier took place in professional sports, for example, the decline in the minor league infrastructure was offset by the increasing importance of the university as a developer of young talent. A similar phenomenon could well occur within the performing arts.

The broader question about quality is whether the growing role of the marketplace in the arts will make it more difficult for original works of enduring value to be produced and performed. As we noted in Chapter One, opinion on this point is divided. On one hand, advocates for the market, such as Tyler Cowen

(1998), assert that by serving a wide variety of tastes, market forces promote innovation across artistic styles. In making this case, they point out that creative geniuses like Shakespeare, Mozart, and Beethoven all had a broad popular following in their day. On the other hand, commentators like Robert Brustein of *The New Republic* already bemoan the destructive effects of commercialism on American theater: "The products of the non-profit theaters . . . have been growing almost indistinguishable from Broadway (and off-Broadway) in their dependence on the box office and in the lowered ambitions of their work" (Brustein, 2000). The truth is, without more data on programming and institutional expenditures, it is very hard to determine the effects of the marketplace on what is produced and performed.

One could argue that the new era will be able to avoid the tyranny of the majority because artists can now directly reach sophisticated niche audiences through computer-mediated communications. But the highly decentralized nature of the Internet is likely to make it more difficult to reach the attention of more than a small circle of admirers.

Indeed, the major problem with such a decentralized distribution system may well be a lack of quality control rather than a lack of quality per se. There will simply be too much material available for consumers to distinguish works of exceptional merit from all the others. To those convinced that the high arts form an aesthetic pinnacle, the new world of the arts that we envision will be inferior because popular tastes rather than true artistic excellence will become the primary arbiter of what does and does not get performed—in the nonprofit as well as the for-profit sector.

Once again, to the extent that midsized organizations offer centers of creativity and innovation, the potential decline of the middle tier could pose a particular threat. The decline of the middle tier could eliminate the set of organizations that provide the R&D necessary for the continuing growth of creativity and innovation in the arts. On the other hand, the niche markets served by growing numbers of small nonprofit and for-profits could serve as incubators of innovation.

Ultimately, of course, the quality of a work of art can only be determined over time. The historical evidence suggests that, during any given period, art of long-lasting value is rare and is often not recognized as exceptional either by the public or by critics at the time it is first produced. It is not unreasonable to assume that the same is true of our time. What is crucial, then, is not *where* a work is first performed but *whether* it is performed at all and thus has the opportunity to pass the test of time.

If exceptional works of art can find expression, then they will be judged, as all works have been, by future generations. Where are such works likely to be performed in the performing arts system of the future? The largest nonprofits, although they feature celebrity artists and grand productions, do not rely entirely on traditional programming. Some of the largest nonprofits, such as the Metropolitan Opera and the New York City Ballet, offer some of the most sophisticated and innovative programming in an effort to educate their audiences and maintain their prestige as leading centers of the arts. It seems likely, however, that such practices will remain the exception rather than the rule among most large nonprofits. In contrast, smaller for-profit and nonprofits catering to specialized niche audiences—although not necessarily amateur organizations—may well be more daring in their programming if they can identify and market to specialized niche markets. The key here is to identify such markets and the products that might appeal to them.

Once again, the university sector may play a critical role in making sure that new artistic voices are heard. Because universities, particularly in their research and training (as opposed to their presenter) roles, are much less sensitive to the demands of the market, they will be better able to foster innovation and creativity. In other words, the university may increasingly serve the same basic research role in the arts that it has traditionally played in the natural sciences. According to the natural sciences model, universities, supported by subsidies from the public and private sectors, perform the basic research that is later supported directly by the private sector after the applicability of the basic concepts has been demonstrated and a market established.

The final criterion for assessing the implications of current trends for the future is how they will affect access to the performing arts. The most important loss of access to live performances will be in those regions of the country that may lose the midsized organizations that now produce professional performances of the high arts. In other respects, however, availability of the performing arts is likely to increase. Technological advances and the expansion of the small nonprofit and volunteer sectors will provide increasing numbers of productions of a growing variety of creative works. Internet-based arts, however, will not increase access equally, since not all people have access to—or familiarity with—the new technologies that deliver these performances.

In discussing the quantity and availability of artistic productions, it is important to recognize that over time supply will respond to increased demand. Thus, future public involvement in the performing arts will be constrained less by supply of the arts than by public interest in the arts—that is, by demand. Indeed, the critical challenge for increasing all aspects of the supply of the arts (quantity, quality, and access) is stimulating greater demand for the arts.

How to address this challenge, however, is not altogether clear. Despite the best efforts of scores of institutions and the investment of countless dollars, the profile of the average audience for live performances has changed very little over time (Schuster, 1994). Moreover, there is a lack of systematic research on what influences people to take an interest in the arts. What we do know, however, is that the more knowledgeable individuals are about the arts, the more likely they are to participate. Indeed, demand for the arts, like that for other leisure activities, increases with familiarity and experience (Kelly and Freysinger, 2000). This finding, however, begs the question of how to increase the public's involvement and familiarity with the arts. Again, the sparseness of the literature offers few definitive clues for how to accomplish this, beyond noting that early exposure to the arts and to arts education at all levels of formal education can have a lasting effect on individual involvement with the arts. Arts education can, of course, take several forms including arts appreciation, educating people who teach art, and training artists. More attention should be given to arts education in all of its forms—particularly in locations where such education is largely undeveloped.

Another option is to attempt to build greater crossover between the public's interests and involvement in the popular arts and the high arts. For example, although American teenagers (the dominant demographic groups targeted by multimedia conglomerates) may have had only minimal exposure to theater and classical music, they are much more likely to have purchased recordings of popular music and tickets to films. While it is not clear how to expand those experiences to the more traditional performing arts, it is clearly an issue that should be given more attention by arts organizations.[1]

CONSIDERATIONS FOR POLICY

The objective of this research was not only to improve our understanding of how the performing arts world operates and where it may be headed, but also to address what this understanding might mean for policy. The arts community has expressly recognized both the need to develop a policy-analytic capability for the arts and the importance of articulating a clearer rationale for a governmental arts policy (American Assembly, 1997). Despite these developments, however, it is doubtful that an adequate framework now exists for setting policy in the arts. Policy, after all, is about choosing the appropriate actions to further public objectives. Thus, a policy framework should be based on a clear understanding of the public interests involved, the roles that government (versus others) could play in promoting those interests, and the strategies that government at every level has at its disposal. The following discussion develops these points and offers some thoughts about the directions future policy might take.

---

[1]Moreover, as we noted in Chapter Four, crossover effects within the performing arts appear to be limited. However, as we also noted, more work needs to be done on this topic.

From a public policy perspective, the critical question raised by this analysis is how future developments in the arts are likely to affect the broader public interest. This is a question that has not been given adequate attention by the arts community. Indeed, as the American Assembly acknowledges, the arts community has traditionally viewed arts policy in terms of its impact on arts organizations and artists rather than on the American public. In response, the Assembly has called for a much more explicit consideration of the public benefits of the arts. We agree. As a first step, the arts community needs to devote effort to demonstrating why the arts should be considered an appropriate subject for public policy.

In this light, we suggest that the performing arts serve three essential functions for society:[2]

1. The arts serve as a source of entertainment, enrichment, and fulfillment for individuals.

2. The arts serve as a vehicle for the preservation and transmission of culture.

3. The arts provide a variety of instrumental benefits for society. These benefits exist at the individual, community, and national level.

The first category recognizes that one of the primary functions of the arts is the value they offer to individuals. Indeed, if there were no private demand for the arts, they would not exist. In this sense the arts are a private good that benefits individuals and, in turn, society. Second, the arts serve as a source of culture in the sense that they incorporate "the best which has been thought and said in the world" (Arnold, 1869). Access to the arts preserves and transmits this culture and thus provides direct public benefits both for current and future generations. Third, the arts provide a wide variety of instrumental or indirect benefits at the individual, community, and national level that are of direct benefit to society in general. For example, at the individual level the arts may promote an openness to new ideas and creativity as well as promoting competencies at school and at work. At the community level, the arts can provide a variety of economic and social benefits, such as increasing the level of economic activity, creating a more livable environment, and promoting a sense of community pride. At the national level, the arts can promote an understanding of diversity and pluralism, reinforce national identity in our cultural products, and provide a source of the nation's exports.

---

[2]The societal interests we identify here include virtually all of the public purposes identified in the American Assembly report, but we have classified them differently.

These public benefits suggest that the public has a stake in what happens to the arts, and they thus provide a rationale for government policy. But articulating these potential benefits is only the first step. The arts community needs to be able to document them—something it has not yet systematically done. Too often, advocates have either asserted their existence or accepted available estimates uncritically. As a result, it is difficult to evaluate and prioritize the various benefits claimed and to develop programs to promote them.

Recognizing that the government has a legitimate role in the arts still leaves two important policy issues to address: first, the role government plays in promoting these interests and second, the strategies it employs to do so. In this context, it is important to recognize the unique nature of America's public-private partnership in support of the arts. Unlike the situation in many other countries, the arts in the United States are by and large provided in the private sector. Only rarely is the government directly involved in the production and distribution of the performing arts[3] and, as we have demonstrated, government financing of the arts is a relatively minor component of total revenues. Indeed, the most important government policy in providing financial support for the arts is the tax deductibility of private charitable contributions—a policy through which individual donors rather than government officials make funding decisions. The public's long-standing resistance to direct government involvement in setting standards for the arts suggests the ambivalence with which the public views a direct government role in the arts.

In a future environment in which the market will play an increasingly important role in determining what art gets produced and distributed, it is appropriate to ask how the responsibility for policy should be divided between the public and private sectors. Schuster (1994) has suggested several roles the government might play. First, government policy might be used to promote market efficiency—that is, to prevent the market from producing less than the "socially optimal" amount of a good. Central to this efficiency argument is the economic principle that whenever social benefits exceed private benefits, the market, because it focuses on the wants of individuals, underproduces such goods. This efficiency rationale is particularly relevant to the instrumental or indirect benefits of the arts, such as increasing the level of economic activity, creating a more livable environment, and promoting competencies at school and at work. It is also relevant to the transmission of culture because the desires of future generations are unlikely to be considered by the market.

---

[3]Even where the government is directly involved in production, as is the case in government-owned facilities, the revenues that support those facilities are often jointly provided by public and private sources.

A second role of government policy is to promote equal access to the arts. Issues of access can arise from several sources, including unequal geographic access to the arts, market neglect of the tastes of minority groups, problems arising from poor education, or income disparities. To the extent that the market fails to provide equal opportunities on any of these grounds, it creates an issue of equity that government policy, in principle, can address. Arguments for government support of local arts institutions in small and midsized cities as a matter of civic pride are motivated, at least in part, by this objective.

A third role of government policy is to ensure that individuals have sufficient information to make their consumption choices. Government support for the development of the Internet and related protocols are examples of policies that support this objective. In addition, enforcement of antitrust regulations, particularly when they are designed to prevent the selective dissemination of information by small groups of producers and distributors, also serve this purpose.[4]

A final role of government policy is to promote the arts because they are inherently good for society—a benefit that economists refer to as a "merit good." Implicit in this argument is the notion that the arts promote the public welfare and that the societal benefits of the arts are greater than the sum of the private benefits. Although difficult to measure, examples of such merit goods are the effects of the arts in promoting an understanding of diversity and pluralism and expressing a sense of national identity. Unlike other roles, which call for government intervention only when the market fails to function properly, the merit good argument asserts that the arts are intrinsically worthy of government support. Judging the value of the arts relative to other merit goods, however, requires a much more careful assessment of the public benefits of the arts.

Within this framework, there is still a question about how the division of responsibility for executing these roles should be divided among federal, state, and local governments. Some of these roles, such as implementing antitrust regulation and policies related to the Internet, clearly fall within the purview of the federal government. Others, such as those relating to public access and to the arts' instrumental benefits at the community and individual levels, may be more appropriate for the state or local government. Because preferences for these benefits differ from one part of the country to another, it seems reasonable from a political standpoint for decisions to be relegated to the level of government that is closest to the region the policies will affect. Such a decentralized approach is also consistent with Americans' ambivalence toward a single fed-

---

[4]We recognize that enforcement of antitrust regulations is often driven by other considerations.

eral standard for the arts and their preference for decentralized government decisionmaking.

The final element in a policy framework is a set of guidelines or strategies for choosing among the policy tools available. These strategies can be distinguished in two ways: whether they focus on the supply of or the demand for the arts and whether they affect behavior directly or indirectly. Policies that address the supply of the arts focus on influencing the quantity and quality of arts available principally by affecting the behavior of the suppliers of art—that is, artists and arts organizations. Policies that address demand, on the other hand, focus on increasing the access and exposure of consumers to the arts.

By and large, the focus of most arts policies since at least 1965 has been on supporting the supply of the arts (Chapman, 1992). This focus is reflected at the federal level in the form of direct NEA grants to artists and arts organizations and at the state and local levels both in support for local arts organizations and in the construction of venues to present the arts. However, policies designed to increase the quantity and availability of the arts might be more appropriately targeted at demand. Indeed, if policy discussions are redirected to emphasize the public benefits of the arts, then it seems appropriate to give more attention to strategies aimed at stimulating demand. Both the private and instrumental benefits of the arts are contingent on getting individuals to become involved in the arts—i.e., increasing the number and range of people who participate and increasing the intensity of their participation.

The transmission and promotion of culture, on the other hand, involve not just increasing public involvement with the arts but also ensuring that high-quality work is created and produced. If one believes that an increasing reliance on the market and popular tastes will not support such creativity, a strategy that focuses on artistic suppliers may be more effective. It is important to recognize, however, that such a supply-side approach inevitably generates public controversy about which organizations, artists, and content the government should support. Unlike the environment for the arts in much of Europe, the expenditure of public funds on the arts in America is often viewed as legitimate grounds for criticizing and censoring artistic content.

Regardless of whether policies are focused on supply or demand, policymakers must judge which strategies are most likely to achieve their objectives. In fact, policymakers have a wide variety of strategies, both direct and indirect, to choose from. The most obvious example of a direct approach to support production of art is government grants to the arts; the most important example of an indirect approach is the deductibility of charitable contributions that encourage private donations to the arts. Although these two tools of government policy have received most of the attention of the arts community, there are other approaches. Examples of direct strategies are government funding of arts venues and enforcement of antitrust laws. Indirect strategies include copyright and patent regulations that encourage artists to create new work by protecting their rights to control their work; support for public education, which promotes demand for the arts; and support for development of the Internet as a platform for the arts. These indirect approaches are more diverse, and many of their effects may not be immediately apparent.

Choosing an appropriate strategy for policy, of course, requires an understanding of the objectives that policy is designed to achieve. Given the diversity of participants and the multiplicity of interests that characterize the performing arts system, it will be a challenge for that community to agree on what the objectives of arts policy should be. Consider, for example, that in describing trends in the performing arts, we distinguished among consumers, artists, arts organizations, and funders and noted that each of these categories could be distinguished in a variety of ways. Arts institutions themselves differ along multiple dimensions—including discipline, sector, size, type, and mission. As in other areas of American society, the risk is increasing Balkanization—becoming a nation of niche markets and splintering interest groups—which makes it increasingly difficult to articulate the common good.

Despite the absence of a policy framework and a clear set of policy goals, we believe the analysis presented in this report offers a direction for arts policy—a subject to which we now turn. As we noted above, the central policy issue over the past few decades has been the level of direct federal support for the arts. We believe this focus is misplaced. Although federal funding for the arts has clear symbolic importance as a signal of the arts' public legitimacy, it represents a very small (and shrinking) portion of performing arts organizations' revenues. Second, the federal government's indirect financial support for the arts through the deductibility of charitable contributions is much more important financially than its direct subsidies. Third, direct federal funding of the arts brings with it increased pressures for artistic standards and cries of outrage from vocal citizens who are offended by specific works of art. Finally, battles over federal funding have diverted energy and attention from other issues that are appropriate to the new era of the performing arts we have delineated in this report.

We believe more attention should be given to policy strategies that focus on stimulating demand for the arts. This focus is consistent with the recognition of the need to emphasize the public benefits of the arts and with the increasing role that public demand will play in determining what art gets produced and distributed. Efforts to diversify and broaden arts audiences are also less likely to be subject to the criticisms that have been raised about public subsidies going to arts organizations whose consumers are, on average, more affluent than the public at large. Strategies that focus on stimulating demand are also more likely to increase the quantity, accessibility, and diversity of arts—that is, to expand the market for the arts—than are policies directed largely at supply. Other important issues—such as technological change, increasing concentration in the commercial performing arts sector, uncertainty surrounding intellectual property laws, and a potential decline in employment opportunities for new artists—have been largely relegated to the periphery of policy discussions. It is time to address them more directly, formulate policy objectives, and assess policy options. Finally, in an arts environment in which private actors will continue to have a major role in determining the future course of events, governmental strategies that rely primarily on direct actions to shape private behavior may not be adequate. Instead, we suggest that the arts policy community explore more creative ways in which government policy can provide incentives that encourage arts organizations and others to support innovative programming, to hire and train new artists, and to increase public involvement in their activities. All these issues will require future research and data collection, as we suggest below.

RECOMMENDATIONS FOR FUTURE RESEARCH

Throughout this report, we have emphasized the limitations of the data and research on the arts. Here we recommend specific areas in which further data collection and research would be particularly useful. Given the relatively undeveloped state of research on the arts (at least in comparison with such areas as education and health care), it is important to set priorities to focus resources where they can be most effective.

We have called for more attention to policies that stimulate public involvement in the arts rather than focusing exclusively on promoting supply of the arts. Little research has been done, however, on how interest in the arts develops, either in general or in specific disciplines, or why people choose certain forms of participation. Most studies of demand have been based on cross-sectional surveys of the national population and focus on estimating levels and correlates of participation. Such studies fail to address the process through which tastes for art are formed or how those tastes can be influenced. We recommend future research in this area. It would be particularly useful to develop and test models that explain how tastes for the arts are formed and how they change—and to conduct this research in such a way that it can help inform policy and help arts practitioners who are trying to extend the reach of artistic programs in their own communities.[5] Future research should also examine the role of education in general, and arts education in particular, in the formation of artistic tastes.

---

[5]See McCarthy and Jinnett (2001) for a discussion of how increased understanding of the decisionmaking process can be used to influence participation behavior.

Our recommendation that arts policy focus more on addressing demand for the arts reflects the importance that we and others place on the public benefits of the arts. Despite recent efforts to articulate the importance of these benefits, however, no systematic study exists that documents what we know about those benefits or how they relate to arts participation behavior. As a result, it is difficult to evaluate the benefits claimed by arts advocates, much less to draw lessons that will help design effective programs to promote these benefits. What is needed is a systematic analysis of the evidence that exists about the benefits of the arts and how these benefits are related to patterns of arts participation.

As we suggested in Chapter Five, although artists are at the center of the creative process, we probably know less about them than about any other part of the performing arts environment. For example, we know that a simple dichotomy between artists who pursue their art on a vocational basis and those for whom it is an avocation greatly oversimplifies reality, but we do not have enough information about artists' career patterns, earnings, skill levels, and employment conditions to make finer distinctions. We also know very little about how the institutions and sectors in which artists work affect their employment conditions and career patterns. As a result, although we know that the number of self-defined artists appears to be increasing and that more artists appear to be pursuing their art on an avocational basis, we cannot make any definitive statements about what this might mean for artists' employment prospects or working conditions. Most important, we cannot assess what such changes imply for the quality, quantity, and availability of the performing arts.

The major constraint on improving our knowledge of these issues is the absence of data. As we noted in Chapter Five, the basic source of data on artists is the Decennial Census of Population. But Census data on artists rely on self-definition; fail to distinguish among work done as a performer, other arts-related employment, and non-arts employment; and contain very little information about employers and virtually none on career dynamics. Although some data exist on such issues, they are neither comprehensive nor systematic. We believe that this situation is unlikely to improve dramatically until better data are collected. In particular, we recommend that systematic employment data be collected that distinguish among the different categories of employment (performing, other arts-related, and non-arts) and describe in sufficient detail the characteristics of employers to which the employment conditions pertain. We also believe that longitudinal data are needed on such elements of the career process as training and experience, career motivations, employment patterns, and institutional experience and how these factors have changed over time.

In discussing how the characteristics and financing of arts organizations have been changing, we pointed out several gaps in our existing knowledge. We noted, for example, that the major sources of information on the organizational and financial characteristics of arts organizations, namely, the Economic Census and IRS Form 990 data, are much more likely to capture large than small nonprofit organizations and typically contain almost no information on organizations in the volunteer sector. This selectivity is particularly troubling with respect to the volunteer sector, which appears to be an order of magnitude larger than the large nonprofit sector and is growing rapidly. A more accurate description of the trends affecting the performing arts system will require a dedicated data-gathering effort focused on very small performing arts groups—especially those in the volunteer sector.[6]

A second major gap in our knowledge of arts organizations is the absence of systematic information about institutional expenditures. Although we are able to determine the amount and sources of revenues for nonprofit organizations over time, and thus determine that the earnings gap facing nonprofits appears to be relatively stable, a more complete picture of their financial situation (as well as that of the for-profit sector) requires information on expenditures. In fact, a true test of Baumol and Bowen's cost disease hypothesis requires such information. The absence of expenditure (and cost) data also hampers any discussion of the strategies nonprofit and for-profit firms are employing to deal with changing financial pressures.

Although proprietary concerns limit the willingness of for-profit firms to disclose more complete information about their revenues and expenditures, more could and should be done to collect systematic information on nonprofit arts organizations' financial situation. Indeed, The Ford Foundation conducted a systematic study of a sample of arts organizations in the 1970s (The Ford Foundation, 1974) and that study could be used as a model for future data gathering and research.

Finally, we recommend systematic collection of information on organizational programming and output. As we noted in our discussion of the changing organizational structure of the arts (Chapter Six), we were unable to determine whether the declining average size of most nonprofit arts organizations is a product of the entry of new firms or reductions in size of existing firms. Similarly, in discussing changes in programming strategies of arts organizations, we were forced to rely on anecdotal and specialized studies of existing institutions rather than systematic data on actual programming. In this case, unlike several

---

[6]Important efforts are already under way in this area, such as the Unified Database of Arts Organizations, which is being constructed through the joint efforts of the Urban Institute's National Center for Charitable Statistics (NCCS), the NEA, and NASAA; and the National and Local Profiles of Cultural Support project, which is being cosponsored by The Pew Charitable Trusts, Americans for the Arts, and the Arts Policy and Administration Program of Ohio State University.

others, the problem may stem less from the absence of such data than from the way existing data are collected and maintained by service organizations. Some service organizations collect information on programming and output but generally do not report that information. Although more systematic procedures could be used in collecting and compiling such information, the organizations involved will need to be convinced that there are benefits to doing so. We recommend that this case be made.

Alper, Neil O., and Gregory H. Wassall, *More Than Once in a Blue Moon: Multiple Jobholdings by American Artists*, National Endowment for the Arts, Santa Ana, CA: Seven Locks Press, 2000.

Alper, Neil O., Gregory H. Wassall, Joan Jeffri, et al., *Artists in the Work Force: Employment and Earnings 1970 to 1990*. NEA Research Division Report No. 37, Washington, DC: National Endowment for the Arts, 1996.

American Assembly, *The Arts and the Public Purpose*, final report of the 92nd American Assembly, American Assembly, Columbia University, New York, 1997, pp. 64–70.

Americans for the Arts, "Highlights from a Nationwide Survey of the Attitudes of the American People Toward the Arts," prepared for the American Council for the Arts, The National Assembly of Local Arts Agencies, conducted by Louis Harris, Vol. 7, 1996.

Arnold, Matthew, *Culture and Anarchy: An Essay in Political and Social Criticism* (1869), edited with an introduction by J. Dover Wilson, Cambridge, UK: Cambridge University Press, 1960.

Arthurs, Alberta, and Frank Hodsoll, "The Importance of the Arts Sector: How It Relates to the Public Sector," *Journal of Arts Management, Law, and Society*, Summer 1998, pp. 102–108.

Association of Performing Arts Presenters, *1995 Profile of Member Organizations*, Washington, DC: APAP, 1995.

Balfe, Judith H., "The Baby-Boom Generation: Lost Patrons, Lost Audience?" In Margaret J. Wyszomirski and Pat Clubb, eds., *The Cost of Culture: Patterns and Prospects of Private Arts Patronage*, New York: ACA Books, 1989.

Balfe, Judith H., and Monnie Peters, "Public Involvement in the Arts," in Joni M. Cherbo and Margaret J. Wyszomirski, eds., *The Public Life of the Arts in America*, New Brunswick, NJ: Rutgers University Press, 2000, pp. 81–107.

Baumol, William J., "Children of the Performing Arts, the Economic Dilemma: The Climbing Costs of Health Care and Education," *Journal of Cultural Economics*, Vol. 20, 1996, pp. 183–206.

Baumol, William, and Hilda Baumol, "The Future of One Theater and the Cost Disease of the Arts," in M. A. Hendon, J. F. Richardson, and W. S. Hendon, *Bach and the Box: The Implications of Television on the Performing Arts*, Akron, OH: The Association for Cultural Economics, 1985a.

Baumol, William, and Hilda Baumol, "On the Cost Disease and Its True Policy Implications for the Performing Arts," in D. Greenaway and G. K. Shaw, eds., *Public Choice, Public Finance, and Public Policy: Essays in Honor of Alan Peacock*, London: Basil Blackwell, 1985b.

Baumol, William, and Hilda Baumol, *The Impact of the Broadway Theatre on the Economy of New York City: A Study for the League of New York Theatres and Producers*, New York: League of New York Theatres and Producers, 1977.

Baumol, William J., and William G. Bowen, *Performing Arts—The Economic Dilemma: A Study of Problems Common to Theater, Opera, Music, and Dance*, New York: The Twentieth Century Fund, 1966.

Beene, Melanie, and Associates, *Autopsy of an Orchestra: An Analysis of Factors Contributing to the Bankruptcy of the Oakland Symphony Orchestra Association*, San Anselmo, CA: Melanie Beene, January 1988.

Bergonzi, Louis, and Julia Smith, *Effects of Arts Education on Participation in the Arts*, Washington, DC: National Endowment for the Arts, 1996.

Blau, Judith R., L. Newman, and Joseph E. Schwartz, "Internal Economics of Scale in Performing Arts Organizations," *Journal of Cultural Economics*, Vol. 10, No. 1, June 1986, pp. 63–75.

Bowles, Eleanor, *Cultural Centers of Color: Report on a National Survey*, Washington, DC: National Endowment for the Arts, 1992.

Brooks, Arthur C., "The 'Income Gap' and the Health of the Arts Nonprofits: Arguments, Evidence, and Strategies," *Nonprofit Management and Leadership*, Vol. 10, No. 3, 2000a.

Brooks, Arthur C., "Is There a Dark Side to Government Support for Nonprofits?" *Public Administration Review*, Vol. 60, No. 3, 2000b, pp. 211–218.

Brooks, Arthur C., "Government Subsidies Taking Toll on Nonprofits' Private Donations," *Atlanta Journal-Constitution*, July 2, 2000c, p. B4.

Brooks, Arthur C., *Economic Strategies for Orchestras,* Evanston, IL: Symphony Orchestra Institute, March 1997.

Brooks, Arthur C., *Concert Fee Determination: A Game-Theoretic Approach*, Boca Raton, FL: Florida Atlantic University (Master's Thesis), 1994.

Brustein, Robert, "Requiem," *The New Republic*, March 27, 2000.

Brustein, Robert, "The Death of the Collective Ideal," *The New Republic*, September 11, 1993. http://www.tnr.com/091800.html.

Brustein, Robert, "The War on the Arts," *The New Republic*, Vol. 207, September 7, 1992, pp. 11–12.

Butsch, Richard, *The Making of American Audiences: From Stage to Television, 1750–1990*, Cambridge, UK: Cambridge University Press, 2000.

Carter, Bill, "At T.V. Bazaar, U.S. Companies Look to Buy, Not Just Sell," *The New York Times*, October 9, 2000.

Caves, Richard F., *Creative Industries*, Cambridge, MA: Harvard University Press, 2000.

Chamber Music America, *Chamber Music in America: Status of the National Chamber Music Field, A Working Paper*, New York: Chamber Music America, 1992.

Chapman, Laura, "Arts Education as a Political Issue: The Federal Legacy," in Ralph A Smith and Ronald Berman, eds., *Public Policy and the Aesthetic Interest: Critical Essays on Defining Cultural and Educational Relations*, Urbana, IL: University of Illinois Press, 1992, pp. 119–136.

Chartrand, Harry H., "Copyright C.P.U.: Creators, Proprietors, and Users," *Journal of Arts Management, Law, and Society*, Vol. 30, No. 3, Fall 2000, pp. 209–240.

Cherbo, Joni M., *Creative Synergy: Commercial and Nonprofit Live Theater in America*, Ohio State University Arts Policy and Administration Program Working Paper No. 3, April 1999.

Cherbo, Joni M., and Margaret J. Wyszomirski, "Mapping the Public Life of the Arts in America," in Joni M. Cherbo and Margaret J. Wyszomirski, eds., *The Public Life of the Arts in America*, New Brunswick, NJ: Rutgers University Press, 2000.

Cheskin, Irving W., "The 'Taxpaying' Theater: How Has It Fared During Inflation?" in Hilda Baumol and William J. Baumol, eds., *Inflation and the Performing Arts*, New York: New York University Press, 1984.

Cobb, Nina K., *Looking Ahead: Private Sector Giving to the Arts and the Humanities*, Washington, DC: President's Committee on the Arts and the Humanities, 1996.

Colonna, Carl M., "The Economic Contribution of Volunteerism Toward the Value of Our Cultural Inventory," *Journal of Cultural Economics*, Vol. 19, No. 4, 1995, pp. 341–350.

Cowan, C. Lynn, "Second Homes: Multiple Bases for Performing Arts Organizations," *Journal of Arts Management, Law, and Society*, Vol. 17, No. 1, 1987, pp. 23–36.

Cowen, Tyler, *In Praise of Commercial Culture*, Cambridge, MA: Harvard University Press, 1998.

Dance Magazine. See "Pas de Deux: Capezio, NYCB."

Denisoff, Serge R., *The Popular Record Industry*, New Brunswick, NJ: Transaction Books, 1975.

Deveaux, Scott, *Jazz in America: Who's Listening?* Washington, DC: National Endowment of the Arts, 1994.

DiMaggio, Paul J., "Decentralization of Arts Funding from the Federal Government to the States," in Stephen Benedict, ed., *Public Money and the Muse: Essays on Government Funding for the Arts*, New York: W. W. Norton Company, 1991.

DiMaggio, Paul J., "Cultural Entrepreneurship in 19th Century Boston," in Paul J. DiMaggio, ed., *Nonprofit Enterprise in the Arts: Studies in Mission and Constraint*, New York: Oxford University Press, 1986.

DiMaggio, Paul J., "The Nonprofit Instrument and the Influence of the Marketplace on Policies in the Arts," in *The Arts and Public Policy in the United States*, Prentice-Hall for The American Assembly, Englewood Cliffs, NJ: Columbia University, 1984.

DiMaggio, Paul J., "Cultural Entrepreneurship in Nineteenth-Century Boston," in *Media, Culture and Society*, Vol. 4, 1982, pp. 33–50.

Donnat, Oliver, *Les Amateurs: Enquete sur les activities artistiques des Francais*, Paris: Documentation Francaise, 1996.

Dunn, Donald H., "Unions Are Losing Their Star Billing on Broadway," *Business Week*, November 26, 1984, p. 62.

Economic Report of the President, *Inequality of Economic Rewards*, Washington, DC: United States Government Printing Office, 1997, pp. 163–188.

Ellis, Diane C., and John C. Beresford, *Trends in Artists' Occupations: 1970–1990*, Washington, DC: NEA Research Division, 1994.

Feist, Andrew, and Robert Hutchison, *Amateur Arts in the UK*, London: Policy Studies Institute, 1991.

Filer, Randall K., "The 'Starving Artist'—Myth or Reality? Earnings of Artists in the United States," *Journal of Political Economy*, Vol. 94, No. 1, February 1986, pp. 56–75.

The Ford Foundation, *The Finances of the Performing Arts*, New York: Ford Foundation, Vols. 1 and 2, 1974.

Fowler, Charles, "The New Arts Education," *College Music Symposium*, Vol. 16, 1976, pp. 19–24.

Frank, Robert H., and Philip J. Cook, *The Winner-Take-All Society: How More and More Americans Compete for Ever Fewer and Bigger Prizes, Encouraging Economic Waste, Income Inequality, and an Impoverished Cultural Life*, New York: Free Press, 1995.

Frith, Simon, "Art Versus Technology—The Strange Case of Popular Music," *Media, Culture and Society*, Vol. 8, No. 3, 1986, pp. 263–279.

Froelich, Karen A., and Terry W. Knoepfle, "IRS 990 Data: Fact or Fiction?" *Nonprofit and Voluntary Sector Quarterly*, Vol. 25, No. 1, March 1996, pp. 40–53.

Garvin, David A., "Blockbusters: The Economics of Mass Entertainment," *Journal of Cultural Economics*, Vol. 5, No. 1, June 1981, pp. 1–20.

Gomes, Lee, "MP3 Is Transforming the Way Bands Build a Following; and the Way Record Companies Find Talent," *The Wall Street Journal*, March 20, 2000, p. R14.

Hall, Peter D., "A Historical Overview of the Private Nonprofit Sector," in Walter W. Powell, ed., *The Nonprofit Sector: A Research Handbook*, New Haven, CT: Yale University Press, 1987.

Hamilton, Marci, "The Story Behind the MP3.com Judgement," *Findlaw's Legal Commentary*, November 23, 2000.

Hansmann, Henry, "Economic Theories of Nonprofit Organizations," in Walter W. Powell, ed., *The Nonprofit Sector: A Research Handbook*, New Haven, CT: Yale University Press, 1987.

Hansmann, Henry, "Nonprofit Enterprise in the Performing Arts," *Bell Journal of Economics*, Vol. 12, No. 2, 1981, pp. 341–361.

Harris, Neil, *Public Subsidies and American Art*, Seattle, WA: Grantmakers in the Arts, October 1995.

Heilbrun, James, "Empirical Evidence of a Decline in Repertory Diversity Among American Opera Companies 1991/92 to 1997/98," *Journal of Cultural Economics*, Vol. 25, 2001a, pp. 63–72.

Heilbrun, James, "A Correction to Hilda and William Baumol's Paper 'The Future of One Theater and the Cost Disease of the Arts,'" *Journal of Cultural Economics*, Vol. 25, 2001b, pp. 149–150.

Heilbrun, James, and Charles M. Gray, *The Economics of Art and Culture: An American Perspective*, Cambridge, UK: Cambridge University Press, 1993.

Hirsch, Paul, M., "Processing Fads and Fashions: An Organization-Set Analysis of Cultural Industry Systems," in Simon Frith and Andrew Goodwin, eds., *On Record: Rock, Pop, and the Written Word*, New York: Routledge, 1990. Originally published in 1972.

Holak, Susan L., et al., "Analyzing Opera Attendance: The Relative Impact of Managerial and Environmental Variables," *Empirical Studies of the Arts*, Vol. 4, No. 2, 1986.

Jeffri, Joan, *Information on Artists 2*, New York: Research Center for Arts and Culture, Columbia University, 1998.

Jeffri, Joan, *The Emerging Arts: Management, Survival, and Growth*, New York: Praeger Publishers, 1980.

Johnson, Lawrence B., "St Louis Symphony Orchestra: Accord Despite a Fiscal Sour Note," *The New York Times*, October 15, 2000.

Kartunnen, Sari, *Professionalisation Through Social Closure in the Arts*, paper presented to the International Sociological Association, 1998.

Keegan, Carol, *Public Participation in Classical Ballet: A Special Analysis of the Ballet Data Collected in the 1982 and 1985 Surveys of Public Participation in the Arts*, Washington, DC: National Endowment for the Arts, 1987.

Kelly, John R., and Valeria J. Freysinger, *21st Century Leisure: Current Issues*, Boston: Allyn & Bacon, 2000.

Kingma, B. R., "An Accurate Measure of the Crowd-Out Effect, Income Effect, and Price Effect for Charitable Contributions," *Journal of Political Economy*, Vol. 97, 1989, pp. 1197–1207.

Kozinn, Allan, "Classical Concerts and Recordings Seek Audience on the Web," *New York Times*, June 13, 2000.

Kreidler, John, "Leverage Lost: The Nonprofit Arts in the Post-Ford Era," *Journal of Arts Management, Law, and Society*, Vol. 26, No. 2, 1996, pp. 79–100.

Landesman, Rocco, "Broadway: Devil or Angel for Nonprofit Theater? A Vital Movement Has Lost Its Way," *The New York Times*, June 4, 2000.

Lange, Mark D., William A. Luksetich, and Philip Jacobs, "Managerial Objectives of Symphony Orchestras," *Managerial and Decision Economics*, Vol. 7, 1986, pp. 273–278.

Larson, Gary O., *American Canvas: An Arts Legacy for Our Communities*, Washington, DC: Office of Policy, Research and Technology, National Endowment for the Arts, 1997.

Lemmons, Jack R., *American Dance 1992: Who's Watching? Who's Dancing?* Washington, DC: National Endowment for the Arts, 1966.

Leonhard, Charles, *Status of Arts Education in American Public Schools*, Washington, DC: National Endowment for the Arts, 1991.

Levine, Lawrence W., *Highbrow/Lowbrow: The Emergence of Cultural Hierarchy in America*, Cambridge, MA: Harvard University Press, 1988.

Litman, Jessica, "Revising Copyright Law for the Information Age," *Oregon Law Review*, Vol. 75, No. 19, 1996. http://wwwsecure.law.cornell.edu/commentary/intelpro/litrvtxt.htm.

Love, Jeffrey, *Patterns of Multiple Participation in the Arts: An Analysis of 1982, 1985, and 1992 SPPA Data*, Washington, DC: National Endowment for the Arts, 1995.

McCarthy, Kevin F., and Kimberly Jinnett, *A New Framework for Building Participation in the Arts*, Santa Monica, CA: RAND, MR-1323-WRDF, 2001.

McCarthy, Kevin F., Elizabeth H. Ondaatje, and Laura Zakaras, *Guide to the Literature on Participation in the Arts*, Santa Monica, CA: RAND, MR-1322-WRDF, 2001.

McCarthy, Kevin F., and Georges Vernez, *The Costs of Immigration to Taxpayers: Analytical and Policy Issues*, Santa Monica, CA: RAND, MR-705-FF/IF, 1996.

Menger, Pierre-Michel, "Artistic Labor Markets and Careers," *American Review of Sociology*, Vol. 25, 1999.

Midgette, Anne, "For Singers, a New American Way," *The New York Times*, July 2, 2000.

Miller, Russell, and Roger Boar, *The Incredible Music Machine*, London: Quartet Books Limited, 1981.

Moore, Thomas G., *The Economics of the American Theater*, Durham, NC: Duke University Press, 1968.

Music Educators National Conference, "K–12 Arts Education in the United States: Present Context," *Future Needs*, 1986, p. 10.

Myers, David E., and Arthur C. Brooks, "Policy Issues Connecting Music Education and Arts Education," in Richard J. Colwell and Carol P. Richardson, eds., *Second Handbook of Research on Music Teaching and Learning*, London: Oxford University Press (forthcoming).

National Center for Charitable Statistics, *Guide to Using NCCS Data*, available on the web at http://nccs.urban.org/guide.htm/, 2001.

National Endowment for the Arts, *1997 Survey of Public Participation in the Arts*, NEA Research Division Report No. 39, Washington, DC: National Endowment for the Arts, 1998a.

National Endowment for the Arts, *Theaters Report 22% Growth in Economic Census: 1987–1992*, NEA Research Division Note No. 66, Washington, D.C.: NEA, 1998b.

National Endowment for the Arts, *Dance Organizations Report 43% Growth in Economic Census: 1987–1992*, NEA Research Division Note No. 67, Washington, D.C.: NEA, May 1998c.

National Endowment for the Arts, *Classical Music Organizations Report 22% Growth in Economic Census:1987–1992*, NEA Research Division Note No. 68, Washington, D.C.: NEA, May 1998d.

National Endowment for the Arts, *Visual Artists in Houston, Minneapolis, Washington, and San Francisco: Earnings and Exhibition Opportunities*, NEA Research Division Report No. 18, Washington, DC: National Endowment for the Arts, 1982a.

National Endowment for the Arts, *Artist Employment and Unemployment: 1971–1980*, NEA Research Division Report No. 16, Washington, DC: National Endowment for the Arts, 1982b.

National Endowment for the Arts, *Conditions and Needs of the Professional American Theater*, NEA Research Division Report No. 11, Washington, DC: National Endowment for the Arts, 1981.

Netzer, Dick, "The Subsidized Muse," Cambridge University Press, 1978.

Newhouse, Joseph, "Toward a Theory of Nonprofit Institutions: An Economic Model of a Hospital," *American Economic Review*, Vol. 60, March 1970, pp. 64–74.

Oates, Wallace E., "An Essay on Fiscal Federalism," *Journal of Economic Literature*, Vol. 37, September 1999, pp. 1120–1149.

OPERA America, *Annual Field Report*, Washington, DC: OPERA America, various years.

Orend, Richard J., and Carol Keegan, *Education and Arts Participation: A Study of Arts Socialization and Current Arts-Related Activities Using 1982 and 1992 SPPA Data*, National Endowment for the Arts, Washington, DC: 1996.

Pareles, Jon, "Musicians Take Copyright Issue to Congress," *The New York Times*, May 25, 2000.

"Pas de Deux: Capezio, NYCB," *Dance Magazine*, February 2001, p. 47.

Peters, Monnie, and J. M. Cherbo, "The Missing Sector: The Unincorporated Arts," *Journal of Arts Management, Law, and Society*, Vol. 28, No. 2, 1998, pp. 115–128.

Peters, Monnie, and Joni Maya Cherbo, *Americans' Personal Participation in the Arts: 1992, A Monograph Describing the Data from the Survey of Public Participation in the Arts*, Washington, DC: National Endowment for the Arts, 1996.

Peterson, Elizabeth, *The Changing Faces of Tradition: A Report on the Folk and Traditional Arts in the United States*, NEA Research Division Report No. 38, Washington, DC: National Endowment for the Arts, 1996.

Peterson, Richard A., and David G. Berger, "Reply: Measuring Industry Concentration, Diversity and Innovation in Popular Music," *American Sociological Review*, Vol. 61, No. 1, February 1996, pp. 175–178.

Peterson, Richard A., and David G. Berger, "Cycles in Symbol Production: The Case of Popular Music," in Simon Frith and Andrew Goodwin, eds., *On Record: Rock, Pop, and the Written Word*, New York: Routledge, 1990. Reprinted from 1975 article.

Peterson, Richard A., Roger M. Kern, and Pamela C. Hull, "Age and Arts Participation: 1982–1997," National Endowment for the Arts, NEA Research Division Report No. 42, 1999.

Peterson, Richard A., Darren E. Sherkat, Judith H. Balfe, and Rolf Meyersohn, *Age and Arts Participation, with a Focus on the Baby Boom Cohort*, NEA Research Division Report No. 34, Washington, DC: National Endowment for the Arts, 1996.

Phillips, Michael, "More Than Four Actors Need Not Apply," *Los Angeles Times*, Calendar Section, March 11, 2001, p. 7.

Pierce, J. Lamar, "Programmatic Risk-Taking by American Opera Companies," *Journal of Cultural Economics*, Vol. 24, No. 1, February 2000, pp. 45–63.

Pincus, Andrew L., *Tanglewood: The Clash Between Tradition and Change*, Boston: Northeastern University Press, 1998.

Pogrebin, Robin, "Theater for Fun and Profit: Producers' Two Camps Remain Uneasy Allies," *The New York Times*, June 15, 2000a.

Pogrebin, Robin, "A Roundabout Journey to Glamour," *The New York Times*, July 27, 2000b.

Pollack, Andrew, "Time-Warner to Acquire Control of EMI Music," *The New York Times*, January 24, 2000.

President's Committee on the Arts and Humanities, *Creative America*, Washington, DC: President's Committee on the Arts and Humanities, 1997.

Putnam, Robert, *Bowling Alone: The Collapse and Revival of American Community*, New York: Simon and Schuster, 2000.

Recording Industry Association of America (RIAA), "Recording Industry Releases 2000 Manufacturers' Shipments and Value Report," February 16, 2001. http://www.riaa.com/pdf/year_end_2000.pdf.

Renz, Loren, and Steven Lawrence, *Arts Funding: An Update on Foundation Trends*, Third Edition, New York: The Foundation Center, 1998.

Robinson, John P., *Arts Participation in America: 1982–1992*, Washington, DC: National Endowment for the Arts, 1993.

Robinson, John P., "A Review: Survey Organization Differences in Estimating Public Participation in the Arts," *Public Opinion Quarterly*, Vol. 52, No. 3, 1989.

Robinson, John P., and Geoffrey Godbey, *Time for Life: The Surprising Ways Americans Use Their Time*, University Park, PA: Pennsylvania State University Press, 1997.

Robinson, John P., et al., *Public Participation in the Arts: Final Report on the 1982 Survey*, Washington, DC: National Endowment for the Arts, 1985.

Rosen, Sherwin, "The Economics of Superstars," *American Economic Review*, Vol. 71, No. 5, 1982, pp. 845–858.

Ruttenberg, Friedman, Kilgallon, Gutchess & Associates, *Survey of Employment, Underemployment and Unemployment in the Performing Arts Human Resources Institute*, AFL-CIO, 1977, 1978.

Sanjek, Russell, and David Sanjek, *American Popular Music Business in the 20th Century*, New York: Oxford University Press, 1991.

Schor, Juliet, *The Overworked American: The Unexpected Decline of Leisure*, New York: Basic Books, 1991.

Schuster, J. Mark, "Arguing for Government Support of the Arts: An American View," in *The Arts in the World Economy*, Hanover, NH: University Press of New England for Salzburg Seminar, 1994.

Schuster, J. Mark, *The Audience for American Art Museums*, NEA Research Division Report No. 23, Washington, DC: National Endowment for the Arts, 1991.

Schuster, J. Mark, Alan L. Feld, and Michael O'Hare, *Patrons Despite Themselves: Taxpayers and Arts Policy*, New York: New York University Press, 1983.

Schwarz, Samuel, "Differential Economies and a Decreasing Share of Artistic Personnel Costs," *Journal of Cultural Economics*, Vol. 7, No. 1, June 1983, pp. 27–31.

Scott, A. J., "The U.S. Recorded Music Industry: On the Relations Between Organization, Location, and Creativity in the Cultural Economy," *Environment and Planning*, Vol. 31, No. 11, 1999.

Seabrook, John, *Nobrow: The Culture of Marketing, The Marketing of Culture*, New York: Alfred A. Knopf, 2000.

Siegel, Marcia B., "The Flimsy Vault," *Hudson Review*, July 1977, p. 251.

Smith, David Horton, "The Rest of the Nonprofit Sector: Grassroots Associations as the Dark Matter Ignored in Prevailing 'Flat Earth' Maps of the Sector," *Nonprofit and Voluntary Sector Quarterly*, Vol. 26, No. 2, June 1997.

Smith, Ralph A., "Policy for Arts Education: Whither the Schools, Whither the Public and Private Sectors," in R. A. Smith and R. Berman, eds., *Public Policy and the Aesthetic Interest: Critical Essays on Defining Cultural and Educational Relations*, Urbana, IL: University of Illinois Press, 1992, pp. 137–152.

Smith, Sid, "Chicago's Very Own Joffrey Ballet Launches Its New Era with 'Nutcracker' Staging in Washington," *The Chicago Tribune*, December 8, 1995.

Stebbins, Robert, *Amateurs, Professionals, and Serious Leisure*, Montreal: McGill-Queens University Press, 1992.

Steinberg, Richard, "On the Financial Structure of the US Non-Profit Sector," *Voluntas*, Vol. 4, No. 2, 1993, pp. 199–204.

Stigler, George J., and Gary S. Becker, "De Gustibus Non Est Disputandum," *American Economic Review*, Vol. 67, No. 2, 1977, pp. 76–90.

Strauss, Neil, "Music Mergers Herald a Shift to the Internet," *The New York Times*, January 26, 2000.

Stroud, Michael, "A Music Industry Death Knell?" *Wired*, January 11, 2000.

Tepper, Steven J., *Making Sense of the Numbers: Estimating Arts Participation in America*," Princeton University, Working Paper No. 4, 1998.

"The New NEA Arts-in-Education Program," *Arts Education Policy Review*, Vol. 88, No. 2, 1986, pp. 25–33.

Throsby, C. David, "Disaggregated Earnings Functions of Artists," in Victor Ginsburgh and Pierre-Michel Menger, eds., *Economics of the Arts: Selected Essays*, Amsterdam: Elsevier Science BV, 1996.

Throsby, C. David, "The Production and Consumption of the Arts: A View of Cultural Economics," *Journal of Economic Literature*, Vol. 32, March 1994.

Throsby, C. David, and B. Thompson, *But What Do You Do for a Living? A New Economic Study of Australian Artists*, Redfern, Australia: Australia Council for the Arts, 1994.

Throsby, C. David, and Glenn A. Withers, *The Economics of the Performing Arts*, New York: St. Martin's Press, 1979.

Toffler, Alvin, *The Culture Consumers: A Study of Art and Affluence in America*, New York: St. Martin's Press, 1964.

Tommasini, Anthony, "Inspiring a Turnaround at the Opera," *The New York Times*, May 16, 2000a.

Tommasini, Anthony, "Decline of the Full Recorded Opera," *The New York Times*, January 5, 2000b.

Urice, John K., "The Future of the State Arts Agency Movement in the 1990s: Decline and Effect," *Journal of Arts Management, Law (and Society)*, Vol. 22, No. 1, Spring 1992, pp. 19–32.

U.S. Department of Commerce, Bureau of the Census, *Census of Service Industries*, various years.

U.S. Department of Labor, Bureau of Labor Statistics, *Current Population Survey*, various months.

U.S. Federal Trade Commission, *Record Companies Settle FTC Charges of Restraining Competition in CD Music Market*, Press Release, May 10, 2000. http://www.ftc.gov/opa/2000/05/cdpres.htm.

Useem, Michael, "Corporate Support for Culture and the Arts," In Margaret J. Wyszomirski and Pat Clubb, eds., *The Cost of Culture: Patterns and Prospects of Private Arts Patronage*, New York: ACA Books, 1990.

Vogel, Harold L., *Entertainment Industry Economics: A Guide for Financial Analysis*, 4th ed., Cambridge, UK: Cambridge University Press, 1998.

von Rhein, John, "Classical Music No Longer Fits in a Profit-Driven Cynical Record Industry," *The Chicago Tribune*, May 18, 2000.

Westat, Inc., *1992 Addendum to the 1989 Sourcebook of Arts Statistics*, Washington, DC: National Endowment for the Arts, May 1992.

Williams, Caroline, *Financing Techniques for Nonprofit Organizations: Borrowing from the For-Profit Sector*, Washington, DC: President's Commission for the Arts and Humanities, 1998.

Yoshitomi, Gerald, "Cultural Equity Part 2: Cultural Democracy," in S. Benedict, ed., *Public Money and the Muse*, New York: W. W. Norton for the American Assembly, 1991, pp. 195–215.

AEE-3119